# 110 Real Life English Conversations

ISBN 9798843890865 (paperback)

Independently Published

First printing 2022

**SPECIAL THANKS TO OUR VOICE ACTORS IN THE AUDIO VERSION:**

| | |
|---|---|
| Adam J. Bodnar | Jan Lawter |
| Adam Griggs | Jessica Mullen |
| Anna Fowler | Josh Pederson |
| Calvin Hanson | Kairo Hanson |
| Camille Hanson | Lexsa Hightower |
| Corey Wavle | Maddox Hanson |
| Denise Berrio | Mark Lawter |
| Dylon Parzych | Melodie Aho |
| Edward Simmons | Myles Berrio |
| Gabriel Espindola Rosa | Olivia Perry |
| Gabrielle Godard | Senni Anderson |
| Heather Stromer | Tessa Godard |
| Isabel Seppala | Violet Aho |
| Ivory Hanson | |

# TABLE OF CONTENTS

# Introduction

So you want to learn English? Amazing! You're in the right place.

I've written this book to help you to understand real life English dialogues. This isn't the kind of English that you will find in textbooks, but this is the English that you will encounter in day to day situations in real life. The vocabulary and phrases used in this book is what you would hear if you were living here in the United States. There are 223 expressions used throughout the book.

Every situation is something that you would eventually come across in real life, which is why I used real life English in this book. I actually have used my own life as a reference, so many of these dialogues have taken place in my own life.

If you're uncertain of an expression or vocabulary word that is used, highlight it, and write it in the <u>notes section</u> at the end of the book. Then take the time to look up the meaning. This is how you can expand your vocabulary. If you want to study even more, I have written a companion guide available on my website which goes over the meanings of the 223 expressions plus examples.

These conversations are read by 27 different people. This was intentional. I wanted you to be able to hear a variety of accents that you may come across here in the states. Be sure to download the Free Audio of every conversation in this book!

**FREE AUDIO DOWNLOAD**

## Please go to PAGE 50 for link

# To get the MOST out of this book:

## #1

Listen to the audio

## #2

Write down new words and phrases with the meaning in the back of the book.

## #3

Role play these conversations out loud with a friend.

## #4

Repeat steps 1 & 3 many times.

Repetition is the key to perfecting your English. I recommend for you to focus on one to two dialogues per day. Once you feel comfortable, move on to the next one. As always, don't forget to have fun!

# At the Emergency Room

**Rita:** Please, somebody help me. My daughter hasn't stopped crying for the past hour. Her stomach hurts.

**Receptionist:** I'm sorry to hear that. Please fill out these forms and a nurse will be with you in a moment.

**Rita:** Okay, I filled out all the forms.

**Receptionist:** Okay, can I see your daughter's insurance card as well?

**Rita:** Yes, here it is.

**Receptionist:** Great, I will make a copy of this and get it back to you. Please take a seat and the nurse will be right with you.

**Nurse:** Lynn Smith?

**Rita:** Oh, that's us. Let's go Lynn. The nurse will help you.

**Nurse:** What seems to be the issue today?

**Rita:** My daughter hasn't stopped crying for the past hour saying her tummy hurts. I'm worried. I don't know what else to do.

**Nurse:** Has she had a fever?

**Rita:** No. And she hasn't eaten anything strange either.

**Nurse:** When's the last time she went to the bathroom?

**Rita:** She pooped right before coming here, but is still saying it hurts.

**Nurse:** Let's see Lynn. I'm going to touch your tummy. I won't hurt you. Do you feel this?

**Lynn:** Yes. It hurts.

**Nurse:** I think we should run some X-rays just to be sure.

**Nurse:** Oh yes, there is a lot of blockage in her colon. I will prescribe some medicine to help her. Also, be sure she is drinking a lot of water and eating foods high in fiber.

**Rita:** Okay, when do you think she will start to feel better?

**Nurse:** I would say by the end of the day. If she still isn't doing well in 3 days, feel free to come back in.

**Rita:** Okay, I feel reassured. Thank you so much for your help.

# Calling Customer Support

**Customer Service Agent:** Thanks for calling Duke Energy. How may I assist you today?

**Laura:** Hi, yes. I'm calling because I received my power bill and it seemed high to me. It was double what I have been paying.

**Customer Service Agent:** I'm sorry to hear that. Can you provide me with your account number?

**Laura:** Sure it's 7893472.

**Customer Service Agent:** Laura Parks? You live on 72 West Palm Avenue?

**Laura:** Yes, that's me.

**Customer Service Agent:** Have you done anything different around your house this month?

**Laura:** Nothing that I can think of.

**Customer Service Agent:** And how much was the bill for?

**Laura:** It was $400 and I normally pay $200.

**Customer Service Agent:** That does seem rather high. I will have a service representative come check your meter this week. When would be a good time for you?

**Laura:** I work from home, so any time before 5 pm is okay for me.

**Customer Service Agent:** What's the best number to reach you on?

**Laura:** 808-523-4594

**Customer Service Agent:** Okay, I will have the service rep call you about an hour before they come out. Is that okay?

**Laura:** Yes, that works for me.

**Customer Service Agent:** Is there anything else I can help you with today?

**Laura:** No, that's all, thank you.

**Customer Service Agent:** Thank you. I hope the problem gets sorted out soon. Thanks again for being a loyal customer here at Duke Energy. I wish you a good day.

**Laura:** Thanks, you too!

# Returning a Dress at the Store

**Store Clerk:** Hi, what brings you into the shop today?

**Heather:** I need to return this dress I bought last week.

**Store Clerk:** Do you have your receipt? What seems to be the problem?

**Heather:** Yes, my receipt is right here. I tried on the dress again at home and I wasn't happy with how it looked.

**Store Clerk:** Would you like to have a look around and see if you find anything else in the store?

**Heather:** Not today, I'm late for picking up my son from school.

**Store Clerk:** Okay, well in that case, let me help you with this refund.

**Heather:** Thanks.

**Store Clerk:** Do you have the card the dress was charged to? Would you like me to refund it directly back on your credit card?

**Heather:** I think so. Yes, here's my card.

**Store Clerk:** Okay, that was $108.42 that will go back on your card. Is there anything else I can do for you today?

**Heather:** No, that will be all. Thank you.

**Store Clerk:** Thanks for coming in. Have a great rest of your day.

**Heather:** Thanks. You too!

# At the Dentist

**Dentist:** What brings you in today?

**Bryan:** I've been having a lot of tooth pain lately.

**Dentist:** Can you show me where?

**Bryan:** Yeah, it's this tooth here on the bottom right.

**Dentist:** Let's take some x-rays so I can see what's going on.

**Bryan:** I'm a bit concerned about the cost, because I don't have dental insurance.

**Dentist:** You're a new patient here right?

**Bryan:** Yeah, it's my first time.

**Dentist:** We have a $99 special for first time patients which covers both x-rays and a cleaning.

**Bryan:** Okay, let's do that then.

**Dentist:** After looking at the x-rays, it seems that you have a small cavity between those bottom teeth.

**Bryan:** I knew it had to be something.

**Dentist:** It's an additional $140 to fill the cavity, but you can do a payment plan if you wish.

**Bryan:** I guess I don't have many options. Let's go ahead and get it taken care of so it doesn't get worse.

**Dentist:** Okay, open your mouth wide. I'm going to give you some novocaine to numb the area so you don't feel anything.

# Planning to go to the Movies with a Friend

**Camille:** Hey! How's it going? I really want to see a movie this weekend. Are you interested?

**Calvin:** Maybe, what are you planning to see?

**Camille:** There's a new romantic comedy with Jennifer Aniston. You know how much I love her!

**Calvin:** Yeah, I guess I can go with you. What time are you thinking?

**Camille:** Maybe a matinee. There's one that plays at 4pm. That way we can get the cheaper price and grab dinner after.

**Calvin:** Oh, I actually want to try that new Greek restaurant downtown. Wanna go there after?

**Camille:** Sure, I love falafel!

**Calvin:** Great. Do you want me to pick you up at 3:30?

**Camille:** It's a date!

# Putting the Kids to Bed

**Mom:** Hey, come on kids. It's time for your snack. Do you want apples or strawberries?

**Maddox:** I'll have an apple. But I want it peeled.

**Ivory:** I want oatmeal.

**Mom:** Okay. Kids! Stop playing, your snacks are ready. Come into the kitchen and eat.

**Maddox:** Okay, we're here. We were having so much fun with our new game.

**Mom:** Okay, it's time to brush your teeth.

**Ivory:** Can you put my toothpaste on my toothbrush?

**Mom:** There you go. Maddox! I told you already. It's time to brush your teeth.

**Ivory:** I picked out a book mom. I want this one.

**Mom:** Okay, let me read it to you. I like this book too.

**Mom:** Okay, now it's time for thankfulness. What are you thankful for today?

**Maddox:** Swimming in the pool and eating popsicles at school.

**Ivory:** Mommy and daddy.

**Mom:** Good, I'm thankful for you both too. Now it's time for affirmations.

**Maddox:** I'm strong. I'm brave. I'm creative.

**Ivory:** I'm loved. I'm smart. I'm brave.

**Mom:** Yes you are! Now NO coming out of your room. You already had your snack, you went to the bathroom. Your water is right here. It's time to go to sleep. We have a big day tomorrow.

**Ivory:** I love you mommy.

**Mom:** Love you too. And love you Maddox. Now, goodnight!

**Maddox:** Night.

# At the Beach

**Dad:** Wow, it's a perfect beach day, not a cloud in the sky.

**Son:** Yeah, and I can't wait to go boogie boarding.

**Dad:** We're gonna have fun. Let's put this sunblock on you first.

**Son:** Oh, we should put up our umbrella too.

**Dad:** Do you wanna build a sandcastle first?

**Son:** I guess so. I have a lot of new sand toys.

**Dad:** Here, you can put sand in these buckets. I will go get some water.

**Son:** Wow dad, we're making the biggest sandcastle in the world.

**Dad:** We sure are. Are you ready to go swimming now?

**Son:** Yeah, lemme grab my boogie board.

**Dad:** I'll grab mine too. Those waves are perfect. Race ya to the water!

# Ordering a Pizza

**Jess:** Merrell's Pizza, is this for pick up or delivery?

**Jer:** For delivery.

**Jess:** What can I get for you today?

**Jer:** I would love a large vegetarian pizza, no onions and an x-large meat lover's pizza.

**Jess:** Would you like that to be thin crust or hand tossed today?

**Jer:** Hmm, I'll take the vegetarian with thin crust and the meat one with hand tossed crust.

**Jess:** Would you like any breadsticks or drinks with that?

**Jer:** Sure, we'll take an order of your cheese breadsticks and a 2 liter bottle of coke and also sprite.

**Jess:** Great, so I have a large vegetarian thin crust pizza, an x-large meat lovers with hand tossed crust, an order of cheese breadsticks, a 2 liter of coke, and a 2 liter of sprite. Will that be all for you?

**Jer:** That's it.

**Jess:** That will be $52.75. Would you like to pay now by card or with cash upon delivery?

**Jer:** I'll do cash.

**Jess:** Okay. What's your address and a phone number that we can reach you at?

**Jer:** 127 Windswept Dr Greer. 978-1943

**Jess:** Okay, it will be delivered to you in the next 30-45 minutes. Have a great day.

**Jer:** Thanks, you too.

# Getting Drinks with a Friend

**Camille:** Oh, I love this place. I'm so glad you were able to meet me tonight.

**Marika:** Me too. Work has been stressful, I needed a night out.

**Camille:** I'm sorry. I hope it gets better. What are you thinking about ordering?

**Marika:** I love caipirinha. Maybe I'll go for that.

**Camille:** Oh my gosh! It's been ages since I've had one. Actually, the last time was when we were in Brazil.

**Marika:** Me too actually. Everytime I drink one, I'm transported back to the Brazilian beaches.

**Camille:** I think I'll get one too. Maybe we should plan a trip to Brazil together.

**Marika:** I would love to go back. I actually have vacation coming up in 2 months. I would be down to go.

**Camille:** No way! I'm serious. I'm going to check flights this weekend.

**Marika:** I have friends that we could stay with there too.

**Camille:** We could practice our Portuguese. We have to get acai and pastel too.

**Marika:** Oh for sure. I can't wait. This is going to be so refreshing for me. It's just what I need.

**Camille:** Girl, me too! Now, let's order those caipirinhas!

## DIALOGUE 10

# At the Post Office

**Victor:** Next in line please.

**Madison:** Hi. I needed to send this package out.

**Victor:** Okay, is there anything liquid or fragile inside?

**Madison:** Nope.

**Victor:** Would you like to send it priority mail or normal?

**Madison:** What's the cost difference?

**Victor:** It looks like it is $10.40 to send it priority and it will arrive at its destination in 3 days. Regular mail will be around 5-7 days and it costs $6.70.

**Madison:** Let's just do priority then.

**Victor:** Do you want any extra insurance on this?

**Madison:** No thanks.

**Victor:** Okay, it will be $10.40. How will you be paying?

**Madison:** With my card.

**Victor:** Would you like any stamps today?

**Madison:** No, I'm good.

**Victor:** Okay then, you can insert your card there.

**Madison:** Okay.

**Victor:** You're all set. Here is your receipt to track the package. It has this tracking number here. Have a great day.

**Madison:** Great, thanks so much. You too!

# Getting Pulled Over by the Police

**Officer:** Can I see your license and registration please?

**Kim:** Yeah, here they are. Please don't write me a ticket. I haven't had one in years.

**Officer:** Ma'am you were going 20 miles over the speed limit. I clocked you going 55 in a 35MPH zone.

**Kim:** I didn't realize. I was just trying to make it home. It's been a long day at work.

**Officer:** I understand. Give me a minute.

**Kim:** Please, please, please, don't write me a ticket. I'll be more aware next time.

**Officer:** Ok, I'm letting you go with just a warning this time. But you really need to pay attention.

**Kim:** I will, officer. Thank you, thank you, thank you.

**Officer:** Have a good evening. Be safe now.

# Borrowing Something from the Neighbor

**Camille:** Hey Jan. I am in the middle of baking a cake and I realized that I ran out of flour. Could I borrow a cup from you?

**Jan:** Hey Camille. No problem, just a minute.

**Camille:** Thanks.

**Jan:** There you are. I put about a cup and a half in the bag for you.

**Camille:** I owe you! Thank you so much. We are celebrating Kai's birthday and I don't have time to run back to the store. I was just there.

**Jan:** I understand. You're welcome to borrow whatever you need from me.

**Camille:** You're the best. Are you guys going to come over for a piece of cake later?

**Jan:** We would love to. You know your kids are precious to me.

**Camille:** Aww. Well we'll see you shortly then. 5 pm ok?

**Jan:** See you soon. Happy baking!

## DIALOGUE 13
# Asking about English Classes

**Davi:** Is this the cultural center?

**Woman:** Yes it is, what can I help you with today?

**Davi:** I'm fairly new in town and I heard I can take conversational English classes at the center.

**Woman:** Oh, welcome to town. Where are you from?

**Davi:** Argentina. I've studied English for a couple of years before moving here but I would love to connect with people and improve.

**Woman:** I totally understand. I would love to visit Argentina. Anyways, we have conversation classes every Monday, Wednesday, and Friday evening. One Saturday a month we go somewhere fun as a group, like to the park or beach.

**Davi:** And how much are the classes?

**Woman:** You can pay $50 per month and participate in as many classes as you want. If you prefer to pay per class we charge $8 per class.

**Davi:** That sounds good. How long are the classes?

**Woman:** They are 90 minutes each. The Saturday outing is between 3-4 hours.

**Davi:** When can I start?

**Woman:** We have availability so if you would like you can come by the center and fill out a form and start as soon as this Wednesday evening class.

**Davi:** Thanks so much. I'll do that. I'm looking forward to it.

**Woman:** We're looking forward to meeting you. See you soon.

**Davi:** Bye.

# Booking a Hotel Room

**Receptionist:** The Hilton Inn Miami, how can I help you today?

**Samantha:** Hi. I'm looking to book a room for the weekend of the 14th, just two nights.

**Receptionist:** Okay. For how many people?

**Samantha:** Just 2.

**Receptionist:** And do you want a room with an ocean view or a garden view?

**Samantha:** An ocean view would be amazing.

**Receptionist:** Okay. Can I have your name please?

**Samantha:** Samantha Brown

**Receptionist:** And a phone number for the reservation?

**Samantha:** 703-987-1231

**Receptionist:** Okay. I have you down for an ocean view from the 14th to the 16th. Continental breakfast and free parking on the premises are included with your stay. That will be $289.90 after taxes. How would you like to pay?

**Samantha:** My visa card.

**Receptionist:** The number and expiration date?

**Samantha:** 4564 1289 8921 2121. It expires April 2024.

**Receptionist:** And the 3 digit code on the back?

**Samantha:** 421

**Receptionist:** Okay great. You are all set. Have a great day and we will see you soon.

**Samantha:** Oh, I wanted to see if we could have an early check-in on the 14th?

**Receptionist:** Just a moment. Our normal check-in time is 4pm, but it looks like we will be able to accommodate you at 2pm.

**Samantha:** Amazing! Thanks so much. See you then.

# DIALOGUE 15

# At the Airport

**Ticket agent:** Hi! Can I see your ID please?

**Lily:** Yep, here's my passport.

**Ticket agent:** I see you're flying to Dublin today. How many bags would you like to check?

**Lily:** Just one. I also have my carry on and purse.

**Ticket agent:** Okay, no problem. I have you on a connecting flight through Newark and then it's an overnight flight right into Dublin. You can pick up your bag in Dublin.

**Lily:** Great. Are there any window seats still available by chance?

**Ticket agent:** Let me see...yes there is one but it's near the back of the plane. Is that okay with you?

**Lily:** Yeah, it's okay. I would prefer to have a window seat.

**Ticket agent:** Okay. Here are your tickets. I put your baggage claim receipt with your tickets. Remember to pick up your bag when you land in Dublin. Your gate is A which is up the escalator to the left. Have a good flight.

**Lily:** Thanks!! And the nearest bathroom?

**Ticket agent:** You'll see it on the left on your way to your gate.

## DIALOGUE 16

# Buying Train Tickets

**Ticket agent:** Hi, how may I help you today?

**Jocelyn:** Hi. I need to get on the next train to Paris.

**Ticket agent:** Okay, would you like the speed train or the normal one?

**Jocelyn:** The speed train please.

**Ticket agent:** And is that a one way ticket or would you like to purchase a round trip ticket?

**Jocelyn:** Just a one way.

**Ticket agent:** Okay, there is a speed train departing in 30 minutes from terminal 3. You will arrive at your destination in 3 hours. It's 72 euros.

**Jocelyn:** Great, I'll take it.

**Ticket agent:** How will you be paying today?

**Jocelyn:** I have my credit card here.

**Ticket agent:** Okay, let me run that. Great. Here's your card and your ticket. Is there anything else I can help you with today?

**Jocelyn:** No, that will be all for today, thanks.

**Ticket agent:** Okay, have a great trip.

**Jocelyn:** Thanks, you too. Oops, I mean have a great day!

**Ticket agent:** People always tell me that!

# DIALOGUE 17
# Planning a Vacation

**Calvin:** I was thinking we should plan our summer vacation now. It's already May!

**Camille:** Oh gosh, time is getting away from us.

**Calvin:** Yeah, we've had too many projects going on.

**Camille:** Are we going abroad or staying in the US?

**Calvin:** Definitely abroad, Europe is calling my name.

**Camille:** I hear ya! I miss Europe. We have about 10 weeks. Should we try to visit 2 countries?

**Calvin:** Yeah, what if we hit up Norway and Iceland?

**Camille:** I love it. We've never been to either of them. However, they are so expensive! Can we afford it?

**Calvin:** You're right. What if we go to Eastern Europe?

**Camille:** I've been dying to visit Hungary. I even have friends in Budapest.

**Calvin:** I say let's look into it. We could also try to visit Romania. We've never been there.

**Camille:** True. Okay, you look into flights and I'll check out some housing options?

**Calvin:** Sounds good, we need to move fast if we want to find the deals.

**Camille:** I know. I will put it on my priority list. Once you book the flights, I should be able to find housing rather quickly.

**Calvin:** Yes! I'm so excited.

**Camille:** Me too!

## DIALOGUE 18
# Losing your Job

**Boss:** Hey Val. Can I see you in my office?

**Val:** Sure thing boss, be right over.

**Boss:** You can close the door. Thanks. So as you know, I appreciate all your hard work over the past year. You've really grown a lot and contributed to this company.

**Val:** I'm so glad you noticed. I'm really enjoying my job here.

**Boss:** Unfortunately, our numbers have been way down and corporate is on me to let 10 people go.

**Val:** Oh. Wow. This is unexpected.

**Boss:** I wish there was some way around it Val, but I'm going to have to let you go in 2 weeks. You will get a severance package which should help you for a few months while you look for a new job.

**Val:** I'm trying to take this well, but I really need this job. My wife is pregnant with our third child.

**Boss:** I'm so sorry. I wish I didn't have to do this. I will write you a letter of recommendation as well. Like, I said, this isn't my choice. It's corporate. I have to answer to them.

**Val:** Yeah, I understand. You're a great boss and I appreciate all that you've done for me.

**Boss:** I will continue to root for you, and if anything opens up in the future, you will be the first person I call.

**Val:** Thanks so much. Is that all?

**Boss:** Yeah. Again, I'm sorry for the bad news.

**Val:** Yeah, I guess it's life. What can you do?

# DIALOGUE 19

# Going Trick or Treating

**Mom:** Hey kids. Are you ready? It's time to go trick or treating.

**Maddox:** I'm ready! I love being spiderman.

**Ivory:** And I'm superwoman!

**Mom:** You guys look adorable. Where are your baskets? You need them to carry your candy.

**Maddox:** I already put them in the car mom, let's go! I've been waiting all day for this.

**Ivory:** I have to pee.

**Mom:** Okay, well you better go then. Do you need me to help you take off your costume?

**Ivory:** Yeah.

**Mom:** Okay, we're all good now? Let's go to the West End neighborhood. There are a lot of nice houses there and I'm sure you kids will get a lot of candy.

**Maddox:** Aren't we going with Jax?

**Mom:** Yeah, your aunt is going to meet me there with your cousin Jax and then we will all go together.

**Maddox:** Cool. I wonder what costume Jax is wearing this year?

**Mom:** I think his mom said he was going as a ninja turtle.

**Maddox:** Oh man, I should have done that too and then we would have been twins!

**Mom:** Maybe next year. You will still have fun.

**Maddox:** Yeah, I love Halloween, especially all the candy.

## DIALOGUE 20
# Celebrating Christmas

**Hope:** I'm so excited to be hosting Christmas at our house this year.

**Tom:** Is that why you decorated the tree the day after Halloween?

**Hope:** It wasn't that early, but in part yes. I'm so excited that all 4 of our girls will be home this year.

**Tom:** It is nice. It's been what, 2 years since we've all been together for Christmas?

**Hope:** Unfortunately yes! Why do 2 of our kids have to live overseas? I miss them so much.

**Tom:** I know. Maybe this spring we can look into buying a second home in Europe.

**Hope:** Really? That would be a dream! So the house is decorated. Can you help me wrap the presents?

**Tom:** Sure, how about I put the fireplace on and turn on some Christmas music?

**Hope:** I will make hot chocolate. Let me go grab the stockings too. I wanted to go all out this year and really spoil the girls.

**Tom:** Hmm, I think it's in your nature to always go all out!

**Hope:** True. I can't help it. Since Julie has become a vegetarian, I think I'm going to skip the turkey this year.

**Tom:** You know, I'm okay trying new traditions. What are you thinking of making instead?

**Hope:** Eggplant parmesan for the main meal. You know that on Christmas Eve we always have a smorgasbord after the church service.

**Tom:** That's my favorite. And then of course the gift exchange is always nice too.

**Hope:** This year we can also go to the tree lighting ceremony and caroling right after. I thought it would be special and bring back memories for the girls.

**Tom:** You know, I think this year is going to be a very special Christmas indeed.

# At School

**Teacher:** Hi Polly. I wanted to talk to you for a minute. I know you just transferred to this school last month. I wanted to see how you're adjusting?

**Polly:** At first it was a little hard for me, making friends. But now I've made one, so it's been better for me.

**Teacher:** I'm happy to hear that. And how has the workload been for you?

**Polly:** You mean with my homework assignments?

**Teacher:** Yes. Has it been too much for you?

**Polly:** It's a little more than my old school, but I can handle it.

**Teacher:** Your grades are exceptional, especially in math and science.

**Polly:** Those are my favorite subjects. I think I might need to get a tutor for history and English. They are hard and I don't want to fall behind.

**Teacher:** You can always stay after school for help whenever you need. Are you excited for the field trip to the science museum this Friday?

**Polly:** Yes, I can't wait.

**Teacher:** Great. Well, if there is anything you ever need help with, please let me know. I'm here for you.

**Polly:** I appreciate it.

## DIALOGUE 22
# Catching up with an Old Friend

**Seth:** Hey dude, it's been awhile, how ya been man?

**Tim:** Hey man! It's been good. I'm still working at Apple, but I just got promoted to manager. What about you?

**Seth:** Wow that's great. Yeah, things are good for me too. We just had our 3rd kid last month.

**Tim:** No way man! That's awesome. You have a boy and two girls?

**Seth:** Yeah, I think that's it for us. Three is our number.

**Tim:** I don't blame you. Being a parent is no joke. We have just one son, and we don't plan on having any more.

**Seth:** I hear ya. Do you still have your graphic design company?

**Tim:** I do a few projects on the side, but being full time at Apple keeps me busy.

**Seth:** Totally. Next weekend we're going to throw a pool party at our house. Do you guys want to come?

**Tim:** I can check with my wife, but I don't think we have any plans. Plus little Tucker loves to swim.

**Seth:** Great, well let me know. If you can bring some drinks to share, that would be super.

**Tim:** Sure, no prob. I'll get back with you soon. Have a good one.

**Seth:** You too! Tell your family hello from me.

## DIALOGUE 23
# Birthday Party

**Violet:** I can't believe I will be 10 next week.

**Mommy:** I know. My little girl is growing up. Not only that, it's a very special birthday. You turn 10 on the 10th. It's called a golden birthday.

**Violet:** I should have a golden party then.

**Mommy:** We can do that. How about gold and pink, your other favorite color?

**Violet:** Yeah. Can we have a horse party and my friends can take turns riding my pony?

**Mommy:** Sure we can do that. We can work on your invitations this weekend and that way you can bring them to hand out to your friends at school on Monday.

**Violet:** Okay. Can I have a vanilla cake with strawberries?

**Mommy:** Sure, why not? Plus ice cream!

**Violet:** Yay. Can we do goody bags too?

**Mommy:** Yeah, we can shop for them. What do you want for your birthday this year?

**Violet:** Maybe a new saddle for my pony. And some new art supplies.

**Mommy:** I think we can make that work. Should we do a lot of balloons and a piñata too?

**Violet:** Yes! You have the best ideas mom.

**Mommy:** Well, you're a special girl and I want to make this a memorable birthday for you.

**Violet:** It will be!

# At the Groomers with your Dog

**Isabel:** Welcome! What can I do for you today?

**Ruth:** I'm new here and I'm interested in having my dog groomed.

**Isabel:** Oh great. We have a couple of options for you. I see that you have a small dog. For $55, I can do a bath, dry and brush out, nails clipped, ears cleaned, plus a haircut.

**Ruth:** Do you have a package deal? How long does it take?

**Isabel:** If you buy 5 sessions, you will save $5 per session. If you buy 10, you can save $10 per session. It will take an hour and a half.

**Ruth:** Okay, I think I am interested in buying 5 sessions to start. I plan to come every 3-4 weeks.

**Isabel:** That's great. Unfortunately I am booked up for today, but could you come back tomorrow?

**Ruth:** Do you have a morning appointment available?

**Isabel:** Let me see. Yes, I have one at 9:30.

**Ruth:** I'll take it.

**Isabel:** Great. You can pay tomorrow. I accept credit or debit cards or cash. There is a cute cafe right down the road too, if you want to wait while your dog is groomed.

**Ruth:** Sure, I'll check it out.

**Isabel:** I'll see you tomorrow.

# On the Airplane

**Stewardess:** What can I get for you to drink today?

**Juniper:** Can I get a Pepsi, no ice?

**Stewardess:** We just have coke products. Is a coke okay?

**Juniper:** Sure, that will do.

**Stewardess:** And to eat we have pasta with chicken or beef with vegetables. Which do you prefer?

**Juniper:** I will take the pasta please.

**Stewardess:** Okay, there you are. Is there anything else I can get for you?

**Juniper:** I see the seatbelt sign is illuminated, but I really have to go to the bathroom. Can I still go?

**Stewardess:** If you can wait, that would be ideal. The captain should be turning off the sign within the next 10 minutes.

**Juniper:** Okay, sure. One more thing. Is it possible to get another blanket? I'm freezing!

**Stewardess:** Yes, I will bring that right out to you.

**Juniper:** I appreciate it.

**Stewardess:** No problem. Enjoy your meal!

**Juniper:** Thanks!!

# DIALOGUE 26
## At the Park

**Maddox:** I love this park. It has the best slides.

**Dad:** Yeah, and it's not as crowded in the morning.

**Maddox:** Can we go check out the water fountain?

**Ivory:** I want to ride my bike around the circle.

**Dad:** Okay, but look out for other people.

**Ivory:** I will.

**Maddox:** I'm gonna go on the monkey bars.

**Dad:** I'll be over there on that bench.

**Maddox:** Oh there's my friend Ryan. He's in my class at school.

**Dad:** Why don't you go play with him?

**Maddox:** Yeah, okay.

**Ivory:** I'm done riding my bike. Can I leave it by you?

**Dad:** Sure, go play with your brother.

**Ivory:** I want you to watch me dad.

**Dad:** I can watch you from here.

**Ivory:** No! Come with me.

**Dad:** Okay, okay, let's go.

**Maddox:** Look at me dad! I'm spiderman.

**Dad:** Wow, but please be careful Maddox, you're hanging upside down!

**Maddox:** I will dad.

**Ivory:** See dad? I can do the monkey bars.

**Dad:** Wow, you're so strong. How about 10 more minutes guys, then we can go get ice cream.

**Maddox:** Can we go now?!

**Dad:** Haha just play a few more minutes, bud.

# Eating Sushi

**Fred:** I know you'll love it.

**Annie:** But you do remember it's my first time eating sushi right?

**Fred:** Yeah, I'm so happy it's me who is with you.

**Annie:** So I am clueless, you need to help me order.

**Fred:** Well we can start with edamame. It's an appetizer.

**Annie:** Eda what?

**Fred:** Haha, just trust me. It's amazing.

**Annie:** Okay. So what else do you get?

**Fred:** The rolls here are pretty big. We could each get one and share.

**Annie:** That sounds good. I like shrimp.

**Fred:** You should try the shrimp crunchy roll. It has tempura shrimp with avocado, cucumber, and eel sauce. The combination is divine.

**Annie:** I'm nervous, eel sauce?

**Fred:** You have to trust me, you won't be disappointed.

**Annie:** Okay, okay. What will you get?

**Fred:** I'll get the salmon melt roll. It comes with cream cheese and crab. It's fried and it really does melt in your mouth.

**Annie:** Wow, we'll have to take some photos to document this moment.

**Fred:** I was thinking some Instagram stories.

**Annie:** Oh gosh. Are you that sure I'm going to love it?

**Fred:** I really am. Thanks for being open to trying it.

**Annie:** Well, you've talked it up so much that it would be a shame not to.

# At the Grocery Store

**Helen:** Okay, I think I've checked just about everything off my list. I just need to go get some popsicles for the grandkids. They are coming over tomorrow.

**Jean:** Did you get broccoli for that salad you make with the raisins?

**Helen:** Yup, it's in the cart.

**Jean:** You told me to remind you to pick up buns as well.

**Helen:** Oh shoot. I would have forgotten. Can you go get some? I need one pack of hotdog and hamburger buns for the barbeque tonight.

**Jean:** Sure. Weren't they at the entrance?

**Helen:** Yes. Then meet me at the checkout, ok?

**Jean:** Okay. See you in a few.

**Check out lady:** Hi. How's it going? Did you find everything okay today?

**Helen:** I did. However, I noticed you were out of oatmeal.

**Check out lady:** Sorry about that. If you check back tomorrow we should be stocked up.

**Helen:** Okay thanks.

**Jean:** Here are the buns.

**Check out lady:** Okay, that brings your total to $123.42. Cash or card today?

**Helen:** I have my card here.

**Check out lady:** You can tap, slide, or insert your card there.

**Helen:** Okay. Tap. Hmm, it's not working.

**Check out lady:** Go ahead and try to insert your card.

**Helen:** Oh there it goes.

**Check out lady:** Good. You can take your card out. Here is your receipt. Have a lovely weekend.

**Helen:** Thanks, you too!

## DIALOGUE 29

# Having a Baby

**Nurse:** So do you want to find out what you're having?

**Marge:** Yes, but can you write it down on a piece of paper and put it in an envelope? We're going to have a reveal party tonight. It's our first child.

**Nurse:** Of course. Just lift up your shirt. I'm going to put this gel on your stomach for the ultrasound.

**Marge:** Sure. Oh brr, that's cold.

**Nurse:** Sorry about that. There we go. Can you hear the heartbeat? Everything looks good.

**Marge:** Wow, it's amazing. I can't believe I'm growing a little human.

**Nurse:** It really is a miracle. Congratulations. Here is the envelope with the sex of the baby written inside.

**Marge:** Can I also have the ultrasound photos?

**Nurse:** Yes, I'm printing them off now for you. You can take them home with you.

**Marge:** I'm so excited. I'm going to give the envelope to my sister. She's going to bake a cake and the inside will be either pink or blue.

**Nurse:** What a fun idea. Well everything looks good here. You're measuring right on track. Do you have any questions for me?

**Marge:** Not that I can think of for the moment. I think I'm just so excited. I had pretty bad morning sickness last month, but it's finally subsided.

**Nurse:** That's good to hear. Be sure to take your prenatal vitamins daily and exercise for at least thirty minutes a day.

**Marge:** Yes, I've been very faithful.

**Nurse:** Great. You can schedule your next appointment on your way out. I would like to see you again in 4 weeks.

**Marge:** Okay. Thanks so much. Have a great day.

**Nurse:** You too!

# DIALOGUE 30
# At the Library

**Librarian:** Hi. What can I help you with today?

**Chris:** Hi. My son is interested in finding some books about the natural rain forest.

**Librarian:** Do you want me to show you how to use our computer so you can find them yourself or would you prefer that I show you?

**Chris:** Could you just show me?

**Librarian:** Yes, I would be happy to do that. Right this way.

**Chris:** Thanks. Oh there's actually a pretty big selection. How many books can I check out?

**Librarian:** You can check out up to 20 books and you have 2 weeks until you have to return them again.

**Chris:** Oh wow, that's great.

**Librarian:** Is there anything else I can help you with?

**Chris:** That's all for the moment.

**Librarian:** Okay, just come up to the check out when you're ready.

**Chris:** Will do.

**Chris:** Okay, I think I found what I need.

**Librarian:** Great. You can put them up on the counter. Do you have your library card?

**Chris:** Yes. Here it is.

**Librarian:** Oh, it looks like you have one outstanding fee from the book, "The hope within". Would you like to pay that now? It's $3.40.

**Chris:** Ohhh, yeah. I forgot I had returned that late. Yeah, I will pay the fee now. Here's my card.

**Librarian:** Thank you. Here are your books. They are due on the 25th, two weeks from today.

**Chris:** Sounds good. Thank you.

**Librarian:** Have a great rest of your week.

# DIALOGUE 31
# At the Hair Salon

**Hair Stylist:** Hi, what brings you in today?

**Lane:** I saw your sign that said walk-in appointments welcome. I really need a haircut.

**Hair Stylist:** Well I'm glad you came in. We have one of our stylists finishing up with an appointment and then she will be able to take you.

**Lane:** Great. Do you know if she has time to highlight my hair as well?

**Hair Stylist:** Let me see. No. She has another appointment in 30 minutes. But you can always schedule something if you would like. I'm sure someone can squeeze you in tomorrow.

**Lane:** Maybe I should do it. It's been 6 months since I've touched my hair.

**Hair Stylist:** Do you want to come back tomorrow and cut your hair at the same time? Let me see. We have an 11am or a 4pm time slot available.

**Lane:** I work until 2 tomorrow, so I will take the 4pm time.

**Hair Stylist:** Great. What's your name and phone number?

**Lane:** Lane Sullivan. 424-0921

**Hair Stylist:** Okay. I put your name down. We will see you tomorrow. If you can come back with some photos of the hair color and cut that you like, that will be helpful.

**Lane:** Yeah, I actually have some photos saved on my phone.

**Hair Stylist:** Perfect dear. See you tomorrow.

**Lane:** Bye!

# At the Zoo

**Mom:** I am so happy to take you kids to the zoo today. It's so cool that they are running that special.

**Maddox:** Yeah, kids get in for free.

**Mom:** This zoo is huge, so I made sure to pack a lot of snacks, sunblock, and bug spray. We will most likely be here for 4 hours.

**Ivory:** Yay. I want to see the cheetahs.

**Maddox:** I can't wait. I really want to see the lion and snakes.

**Mom:** Did you know that they just got a new elephant last month too?

**Maddox:** I didn't know. I can't wait to see the llama. It's so cute.

**Ivory:** I love llamas.

**Mom:** Yeah, the llamas are my fave. They are so fluffy and cute.

**Maddox:** I'm hungry.

**Mom:** Already? Didn't you eat breakfast?

**Maddox:** Nope. I forgot.

**Mom:** Well here's a cereal bar. Eat this. And a banana, before the monkey takes it from you.

**Ivory:** Where's the monkey?

**Mom:** It's in the zoo. We're almost there.

**Maddox:** Can I use your phone to take some photos and videos?

**Mom:** Sure, but you need to be careful. I just bought it last week.

**Maddox:** I will. I just want to show them to dad, since he's at work.

**Mom:** Aww, that's thoughtful son.

**Ivory:** Yay, we're here! There's the sign.

**Mom:** Yes, and it looks like it's just opening now, so there aren't too many people.

**Maddox:** Come on Ivory, let's go!

## DIALOGUE 33

# Getting Ice Cream

**Barb:** Welcome to Abbot's Ice Cream. What can I get for you today?

**Jill:** Oh, so many flavors. What's the best seller?

**Barb:** The butter pecan is one of our best sellers. Would you like a sample?

**Jill:** Sure! Can I also try the peanut butter cup?

**Barb:** Sure thing, here you go.

**Jill:** Oh my gosh. Wow, they are both amazing. Can I get two flavors in one cone?

**Barb:** If you choose 2 scoops, yes I can put both flavors in the cone.

**Jill:** Okay, let's do that.

**Barb:** Do you want a regular cone or waffle cone?

**Jill:** Let me try the waffle cone. It looks wonderful.

**Barb:** They are homemade and delicious.

**Jill:** Yum. I can't wait.

**Barb:** Okay, here you are. That will be $6.25. Cash or card?

**Jill:** Here's my card.

**Barb:** Okay, you're all set. Enjoy your ice cream and this beautiful afternoon.

**Jill:** Thanks so much. I'm heading to the park now. Bye.

## DIALOGUE 34

# At the Pharmacy

**Doug:** Hi, I need to fill this prescription.

**Pharmacist:** Let me see. Okay. It will be ready in about 15 minutes. If you want you can browse around the store.

**Doug:** Ok, yeah, I actually need a few things so I will do that.

**Pharmacist:** Great, you will hear your name over the loudspeaker when your prescription is ready.

**Doug:** Alright.

**Pharmacist:** Doug Walker, your prescription is ready. Doug Walker.

**Doug:** Whoa, that was quick. I barely had time to shop. Can I buy these items here too?

**Pharmacist:** You sure can. Oh there is a special discount for toothpaste today. Buy one get one 50% off. Did you want to go grab another tube?

**Doug:** Oh, I didn't see that. Yeah. I'll be right back.

**Pharmacist:** Okay. Do you have your insurance card?

**Doug:** Here ya go.

**Pharmacist:** Okay, so your total comes to $38.41 today. Will that be cash or card?

**Doug:** I have my visa here. Insert. There we go.

**Pharmacist:** Here is your receipt. Come back and see us again soon.

**Doug:** Thanks. Have a good one.

# Snow Day

**Mom:** Well son, it looks like a snow day. No school. There's a blizzard out there.

**Kai:** Yay. What are we going to do? Can we go build a snowman?

**Mom:** I think we need to wait a bit. We can't even see to the end of our driveway because it's snowing so hard.

**Kai:** Oh man. I don't care mom. It'll be fun.

**Mom:** I just checked the forecast. The snowfall is supposed to lighten up in 2 hours. How about we watch some cartoons?

**Kai:** Okay, fine. Can I have hot chocolate?

**Mom:** Sure. If you want, we can also make cookies today.

**Kai:** Yeah, I love making cookies. Can we make the kind we do at Christmas, where we cut them into cool shapes like stars and angels?

**Mom:** With the frosting? The kind we make at Christmastime?

**Kai:** Yeah, those ones!

**Mom:** Sure. Your dad doesn't have work today either, so maybe he can get the snowmobile ready and pull you behind on a sled.

**Kai:** That would be awesome. Can the neighbors come too?

**Mom:** Actually, yes. I already called Cindy and she said her boys would love to play with you.

**Kai:** I love snow days! They are the best!

**Mom:** They are cozy. Now let me get this fire going and then we can either start with cookies or the cartoon.

**Kai:** Cookies!

**Mom:** You got it son. Wow, that snowfall is so magical. I love it.

**Kai:** I can't wait to play in it and catch snowflakes on my tongue.

DIALOGUE 36
# Meeting at Work

**Boss:** Okay you guys. I want to keep this meeting short and sweet so let's get started.

**Employee 1:** What do you have on the agenda for today?

**Boss:** We need to go over budget cuts for the next quarter and review our marketing strategy for the fall product line.

**Employee 2:** I can go over the budget cuts since I'm the head of that department. I have all the information with me.

**Boss:** Great, let's start with that.

**Employee 2:** Okay. So as of this quarter, we are actually right on track. We don't need to make any cuts. However, we do need to be careful with our marketing budget. If we go over $100,000, we will have to make some cuts next quarter.

**Boss:** Oh, that's good news. Good job team. This meeting may be shorter than I thought.

**Employee 1:** I can talk about the marketing strategy since I'm head of marketing.

**Boss:** Go for it. What's the vision with the fall line?

**Employee 1:** Well we're planning on a lot of social media ads, but we really wanted to do some billboards too. We already had the photographer capture some amazing photos with our models. But just with the billboards alone, we're budgeting $150,000.

**Boss:** What can we do to stay under the $100,000 budget so that we don't have to make any budget cuts next quarter?

**Employee 1:** We had planned on running the billboards for 3 months, 4 of them. We could either run them for 2 months or just run 2 of them. Either of those options will give us more freedom in our budget.

**Boss:** Okay. Why don't you strategize with your marketing team and run some numbers. Next week, you can give me your final answer.

**Employee 1:** Will do. Yes.

**Boss:** Great work you guys. Let's go ahead and wrap up this meeting. Keep up your hard work and we will see you for next week's meeting.

# Buying a House

**Real Estate Agent:** Hi. I'm so excited to work with you. Can you tell me what you're looking for in a house?

**Randy:** Yeah. I'm excited too. I'm looking for something with some land. Maybe a couple of acres since I have horses. I would prefer a ranch style house.

**Real Estate Agent:** How many bedrooms and bathrooms?

**Randy:** Ideally 3 bedrooms, 2 bathrooms. I would love an extra room that I could turn into an office for my wife, because she works from home.

**Real Estate Agent:** Okay. And do you prefer new construction or old?

**Randy:** It doesn't matter. As long as the price is right. I really don't want a fixer upper.

**Real Estate Agent:** Okay. Got it. Speaking of price, what is your budget?

**Randy:** To give you a ballpark figure, I would say between $350-$400,000. I already have a pre-approval letter from the bank for a loan of this size.

**Real Estate Agent:** Okay, yeah. That's great you've already been preapproved. As you know, the housing market is hot these days, but I think you have a good budget. Most likely I won't be able to find anything with that many acres of land right in town. But if you're willing to drive 20-30 minutes, I think that will open up some possibilities.

**Randy:** Yeah, I hear ya. The drive is no problem for us. We would prefer to be a little outside of town.

**Real Estate Agent:** Okay. Well, I will be looking, and as soon as something comes up, I will give you a call. You hadn't mentioned if there is a timeframe for buying the house?

**Randy:** We have to be out of our apartment in 3 months. So ideally by then.

**Real Estate Agent:** Great. I'm looking forward to helping you find the perfect house for you and your wife.

**Randy:** I appreciate it. Thank you.

# The Drive-Thru

**Worker:** Welcome to Taco bell. What can I get for you?

**Angelika:** Hmm. I'll take the Nacho Supreme and a bottle of water.

**Worker:** Will that be all for you today?

**Angelika:** Yeah. Actually, can I also get the dessert churros?

**Worker:** Sure. Anything else?

**Angelika:** No, that's all.

**Worker:** Okay, that will be $7.42. Please pull ahead to the next window.

**Angelika:** Okay, thanks.

**Worker:** $7.42

**Angelika:** Okay, here's my card.

**Worker:** There you are. And here is your food. Thanks so much. Have a good day.

**Angelika:** I don't see my water.

**Worker:** Oh I am so sorry. Here it is! Sorry about that.

**Angelika:** It's okay. Thanks. Have a good day.

**Worker:** Bye now.

# Chores

**Rachel:** It's Saturday. You know what that means? Chore day! I'm so glad you didn't have to go to the office today because I can really use your help. We have company coming over for lunch.

**Liam:** Yeah. You do the cleaning the majority of the time, so I am happy to help. Should we divide and conquer?

**Rachel:** If you can clean the bathrooms, I can get started on laundry and the kitchen.

**Liam:** After that I can start dusting.

**Rachel:** Yes. I hate dusting. I will vacuum and then you can mop.

**Liam:** Okay. Don't forget about the outer terrace and emptying the garbage cans.

**Rachel:** Maybe you can do that as well. I will get started on the cooking after?

**Liam:** Deal. Let's crank some tunes.

**Rachel:** I prefer to listen to a podcast. It will help us. You know we have that trip to Japan this summer and we wanted to have some of the basics down.

**Liam:** I'll tell you what. Let's do music for the first hour and then we can switch to the podcast.

**Rachel:** You know it will be harder to hear the podcast when I'm vacuuming.

**Liam:** Okay, okay. Podcast first. Now let's get down to business.

# In the Garden

**Mitch:** Finally spring is here. I'm so excited for our garden this year.

**Avery:** Me too. Grocery prices have gone up so much lately. It will be nice to eat fresh produce and save some money too.

**Mitch:** I'm excited for the kids to help. They're at the perfect ages, 7 and 9.

**Suzy:** We're ready to work daddy. Let's go.

**Avery:** Have fun guys. I'll be doing some chores indoors.

**Dax:** Let's go dad!

**Mitch:** All right guys. I already tilled the soil. I have the seeds here. We're going to plant some tomatoes, cucumbers, broccoli, peppers, and then a lot of herbs.

**Suzy:** What about corn and potatoes?

**Mitch:** You know last year the corn and potatoes didn't grow. Oh but look, I also have some carrot and lettuce seeds.

**Dax:** We're gonna have the best garden.

**Mitch:** I think so. Okay. So we are going to plant the seeds in rows. Let's work together. We will start with the carrots. Do you see how I am doing it, and how far apart the seeds are? Just copy me. Good, good. Exactly like that.

**Suzy:** I want to help.

**Dax:** Here, we're working on the broccoli. Take these seeds. You can put them in the ground.

**Avery:** Hey guys, you've been out here for an hour. Do you want to take a lemonade break?

**Mitch:** That's a great idea. Thanks babe. We've made a lot of progress. We just have the herbs to plant, which I am going to do in those pots right there.

**Avery:** Wow, great work guys. What herbs are we growing this year?

**Dax:** Let me see. We have cilantro, parsley, basil, and mint.

**Avery:** Wow, all of my favorite ones. Thank you guys.

**Suzy:** Daddy said in a month we will start to see the sprouts.

**Mitch:** Yeah. That's the best part. The fruit of our labor.

**Avery:** Your daddy has always had a green thumb!

# DIALOGUE 41
# I'm Sick

**Taylor:** Hey Margo. I'm so sorry but I'm going to have to cancel our date tonight.

**Margo:** Why, what happened?

**Taylor:** I think I'm coming down with something. My head is pounding and my throat is sore.

**Margo:** Oh no. I heard there is a virus going around. Some of my coworkers are sick too.

**Taylor:** Oh man, yeah this sucks. I can't really afford to be sick right now. I have that big work presentation on Friday.

**Margo:** I will bring you some of my essential oils. I also have a secret concoction that I will make you.

**Taylor:** What's in it?

**Margo:** It wouldn't be a secret if I told you right?

**Taylor:** Haha, Come on.

**Margo:** I'm just kidding. It has honey, lemon, ginger, apple cider vinegar, and garlic.

**Taylor:** Oh gosh, that sounds intense.

**Margo:** It works every time. It's packed with immune boosters.

**Taylor:** If you insist. I'm gonna try to sleep now. I'm so tired.

**Margo:** Okay, yes. Get some rest. It's the best medicine. I hope you feel better soon. I'll be over later with my remedies.

**Taylor:** You're the best!

# Shopping for School Supplies

**Mom:** Okay, we're in the supply aisle. What is it that we need?

**Maddox:** I need 4 notebooks, pencils, colored pencils, crayons, and markers.

**Mom:** Wow. I also see here that you need a ruler, calculator, and a case to carry your supplies.

**Maddox:** Can I get the cool superhero notebooks?

**Mom:** I don't see why not. Do you want these matching pencils too?

**Maddox:** Yes. Can I get a new backpack too? My old one ripped.

**Mom:** Oh yeah. I was going to sew it, but I don't think it's worth it. The material is getting so thin.

**Maddox:** Is there anything else on the list?

**Mom:** Let me see. Oh, you also need index cards and dry erase markers. Man, the school should provide some of this stuff. It costs me an arm and a leg just to send you to 4th grade.

**Maddox:** They do provide all the books and a laptop that I can use when I'm there. Plus I can get free hot lunch every day.

**Mom:** That's true. It's a privilege to study son. Some people don't have that privilege.

**Maddox:** Maybe we can send them some money.

**Mom:** You're right. We can do that. You've always had such a generous heart.

## DIALOGUE 43

# Family Reunion

**Trish:** Girl. It's been forevs. I'm so happy to see you.

**Mandy:** I know. First cousins and we see each other once a decade. It's a shame.

**Trish:** I guess that's what happens when you live on opposite sides of the country.

**Mandy:** True. But wow, it's amazing we are all reunited here for grandpa and grandma's 50th wedding anniversary.

**Trish:** Wow, it truly is remarkable. I just celebrated 5 years with Jack last month. I can't imagine 50.

**Mandy:** Have you seen Uncle Mark and Aunt Becky?

**Trish:** Not yet. What about Aunt Patsy and Uncle Ron? They've been living in Thailand for the past 10 years. I can't wait to hear about their life over there.

**Mandy:** Totally. We have so much to catch up on. At least this reunion is a week long. I think we will be sharing a lot of meals together.

**Trish:** We're also going to go on daily boat trips with whoever wants to come and we'll have nightly bonfires too.

**Mandy:** This is legendary. My mom hired a professional photographer to be here the last day. We really need to document this time.

**Trish:** I agree. It only comes around every once in a blue moon.

**GO TO THIS LINK FOR**

**110 FREE AUDIO DIALOGUE TRACKS**

learnenglishwithcamille.com/freeaudio110/

Having issues? audio@learnenglishwithcamille.com

50

# DIALOGUE 44

# Cooking

**Gary:** Can I help you with dinner?

**Anna:** I would love that. I'm making a chicken stir fry with vegetables.

**Gary:** The one with the asian sauce?

**Anna:** That's the one. Can you cut up the vegetables? I'll start cooking the chicken.

**Gary:** Yeah. Don't you need to cook the rice?

**Anna:** I have leftover rice from yesterday that's in the fridge. Fried rice is much better with leftover cold rice.

**Gary:** Oh, okay. So what do we need to cut up?

**Anna:** You can dice some carrots, onions, and broccoli. I will add in some frozen peas.

**Gary:** Done. What next?

**Anna:** I just finished the chicken. If you can scramble three eggs, I will make the sauce mixture.

**Gary:** Sure thing.

**Anna:** It's just garlic, soy sauce, rice vinegar, and some hoisin sauce, but man, it's delicious.

**Gary:** Do we have friends coming over?

**Anna:** Nope, it's just us. But this evening, we're meeting some friends for ice cream.

**Gary:** Yum. Okay. The eggs are done.

**Anna:** Okay, I just need to combine the eggs, veggies, cold rice, and sauce. Can you cut up some scallions and get the sesame seeds out of the cupboard?

**Gary:** Yes. Wow, it smells so good. I'm starving.

**Anna:** Me too! Can you get down the bowls? I will grab the chopsticks.

**Gary:** Let's have some sparkling water too.

**Anna:** Yes, with lemon!

# Baking Cookies with my Kids

**Mom:** Do you kids want to bake cookies?

**Kids:** YES!

**Mom:** Okay, I'll get out the ingredients and you can help me to mix them together. Let me turn the oven on. Okay. It's preheating.

**Ivory:** I want to put the flour in.

**Mom:** Okay, you can do that, but first I'm going to melt the butter.

**Maddox:** Can I put the sugar in?

**Mom:** Yes, we need ¼ cup regular sugar and ¾ cup packed brown sugar. Ivory you mix the butter and sugar. I will put in the egg.

**Ivory:** Okay, can I put in the flour too?

**Mom:** Yes. Also put in this teaspoon of baking powder and the salt.

**Maddox:** I will put in the vanilla.

**Mom:** Good. Let's make sure it's all mixed well. Scrape the sides of the bowl too.

**Ivory:** Can I add in the chocolate chips?

**Mom:** Yes, and then I will scoop them onto the pan and put them in the oven.

**Maddox:** Can I try the dough?

**Mom:** Just a little bit. We need to have some dough to bake too!

**Ivory:** I want some dough.

**Mom:** Okay guys, that's enough. Let's bake them now. In 8 minutes you can have one fresh out of the oven.

## DIALOGUE 46

# At the Bowling Alley

**Bo:** Man, it's been forever since I've bowled.

**Misty:** Me too. At least 5 years. Let's hope I remember how.

**Bo:** Let's go pick out our shoes and bowling balls.

**Misty:** Okay. Oh I think I'll choose an 8 pound ball, this pink one.

**Bo:** I will go for the 12 pounder.

**Misty:** Okay, you're up first. I'll keep score.

**Bo:** Okay, just watch me get a strike.

**Misty:** You crack me up. You got a gutter.

**Bo:** Hey, give me a break. I told you, it's been awhile.

**Misty:** I'm just teasing. Here, my turn.

**Bo:** Hey, not bad. You knocked down 4 pins.

**Misty:** Hey, I got the other 6 down on the second try. A spare!

**Bo:** Not too shabby.

**Misty:** I'm rooting for you. Go for it.

**Bo:** I can't believe it, I got a strike!

**Misty:** How you went from a gutter ball to a strike is beyond me.

**Bo:** Haha, maybe it's my muscle memory.

**Misty:** Maybe. Do you want me to go get us some sodas?

**Bo:** Yeah sure. I'm so glad we came out. I'm having a lot of fun.

**Misty:** Yeah, it's nice to change up our routine.

**Bo:** We really should do this more often!

# A Misunderstanding

**Savannah:** Oh hi Lane. What are you doing here?

**Lane:** Hi! I'm here to babysit your kids.

**Savannah:** Oh my gosh. I think I forgot to tell you that our event was moved to next weekend.

**Lane:** Yeah, I had no idea.

**Savannah:** I'm so scatterbrained lately. Please forgive me. Are you able to come next Friday instead?

**Lane:** Yeah, that shouldn't be a problem.

**Savannah:** Okay. Again, I'm sorry that I got the dates messed up. Here take $10 for your gas and time anyways.

**Lane:** No, it's okay. I actually have some errands to run on this side of town, so I will do that instead.

**Savannah:** Are you sure? I feel so bad.

**Lane:** Yes. No worries. It's okay, really. Don't even think about it anymore.

**Savannah:** You're so sweet. Thanks so much for understanding. I will see you next week hun.

**Lane:** Enjoy your evening.

## DIALOGUE 48

# At the Chiropractor

**Chiropractor:** So what brings you in today?

**Mel:** I was in the garden a lot this week and my lower back is killing me.

**Chiropractor:** Oh, yeah, that will do it. Have you been icing it? Stretching?

**Mel:** Both. I even had to take ibuprofen this morning.

**Chiropractor:** Let me help you out. Do you want a hands on adjustment or my clicker?

**Mel:** I always prefer the clicker.

**Chiropractor:** I remember now. Okay, go ahead and lay down with your head facedown.

**Mel:** Ok. Ouch, even laying down hurts.

**Chiropractor:** Just try to relax. There you go. Oh yeah, I see you are out of alignment. You may be sore after this adjustment. I recommend ice and ibuprofen. If you're still having problems, come and see me for another adjustment in three days. It might take two to get you straightened out.

**Mel:** Okay. I will do that. I also have an anti-inflammatory cream. Would you recommend that I use it?

**Chiropractor:** It wouldn't hurt. Try to take it easy today.

**Mel:** Okay. Thanks again so much.

**Chiropractor:** Don't hesitate to call me if you need anything.

**Mel:** Will do! Thanks!!

# Giving Directions

**Random man:** Hey, could you tell me where Stacy's Cafe is? I've circled this block 3 times and I cannot find it.

**Girl:** Oh. You know what? The cafe changed location last month, that's why. They are actually down 3 blocks.

**Random man:** Ohhh, that explains it. I thought I was about to go crazy. I'm meeting a friend there for lunch. I'm already late and for some reason he isn't picking up his phone.

**Girl:** Oh. I'm sorry. Okay. So walk to the stop sign and take a right on Smith Avenue. You will need to walk two blocks and take a left on Tucker Street. On the corner there is a florist shop. After that, walk one more block and you will see Stacy's on your right. Next to it there is a small boutique called Rose. You can't miss it.

**Random man:** Okay. So right on Smith, left on Tucker, down a bit and Stacy's is on my right?

**Girl:** You got it. It will be under a ten minute walk from here. If you get lost, put Rose boutique in your GPS and you should find it with no problem.

**Random man:** Okay. Thank you so much. I really appreciate it.

**Girl:** No prob. Enjoy your lunch. Stacy's is really good. I recommend her homemade potato soup. It's out of this world.

**Random man:** Thanks for the tip. I might have to try it. Have a good day.

**Girl:** You too. Bye.

# A Rainy Day

**Calvin:** Wow, that rain is really coming down. I checked the forecast and I don't think it's going to let up anytime soon.

**Camille:** I'm so bummed. I had some errands to run.

**Calvin:** Can't you just do them tomorrow?

**Camille:** Yeah, I guess. It's just that I really wanted to get them done. I guess I can focus on some indoor chores.

**Calvin:** That's always good. I think I'm going to finish painting the kids' bedroom today.

**Camille:** Oh that will be so nice to have that project finished.

**Calvin:** I know. It keeps dragging on. But today is the day. It's a rainy Saturday. Let's get some projects done.

**Camille:** You know, you've motivated me. I think I will tackle the kitchen first and then go through the kids' clothes. They're growing so fast. I would like to get rid of the clothes that don't fit them anymore.

**Calvin:** Oh that's a good idea. It always feels good to get rid of things. We have too much.

**Camille:** I know. I swear, living in America does that to you. We consume too much. Let's travel again.

**Calvin:** We can learn to live in America and not consume. It's hard, but it can be done.

**Camille:** Oh my gosh. That thunder was so loud, I thought it was going to knock the house down.

**Calvin:** Yeah, we haven't had a storm like this in a long time. Hopefully it passes quickly.

**Camille:** For real. Well I'm gonna crank up some tunes and get to work.

**Calvin:** Me too!

# At the Paint Store

**Store Clerk:** Hi, what can I help you with today?

**Tammy:** I'm repainting my bedroom. I am looking for some shade of white. I would like something fresh and clean.

**Store Clerk:** Okay, let me take you over to our samples. We have a lot of shades of white.

**Tammy:** What are the best sellers?

**Store Clerk:** Let me pull a few samples for you. Did you want to go home and put the swatch up to the wall or did you want to buy the paint right now?

**Tammy:** I think I need to take it home and see it in my room.

**Store Clerk:** Most people do since the tone can change depending on the lighting.

**Tammy:** Okay, let's see what you have. There are so many to choose from.

**Store Clerk:** I would recommend these 5. They are all best sellers and would go beautifully in a bedroom.

**Tammy:** What finish do you recommend?

**Store Clerk:** Most people do eggshell for the bedroom because you can easily wash off marks on the walls. However, flat paint is very easy to touch up without having to repaint the whole wall. So it's really your call.

**Tammy:** Okay, I'll ask my husband. I actually will buy some paint supplies now.

**Store Clerk:** What do you need?

**Tammy:** I have a paintbrush at home, but I ran out of tape and I need a new roller.

**Store Clerk:** I can get those for you. Anything else?

**Tammy:** Nope. I'll run home now and probably be back in less than an hour. I live just right down the road and I want to paint my room today.

**Store Clerk:** No problem. We'll see you in a little bit.

**Tammy:** Thanks! Bye!

## DIALOGUE 52
# Job Interview

**Heather:** So have you ever worked at a gym before?

**Camille:** Yes, I have.

**Heather:** And where was that?

**Camille:** I worked at Sportsclub for a few years in the city and then I also worked at a local gym for several years.

**Heather:** Okay, great, and you are at least 18 years of age?

**Camille:** I'm flattered. Yes of course.

**Heather:** And if we administer a drug screen or background check, are you okay with that?

**Camille:** Yes, sure.

**Heather:** All right. So our hours of operation are 8am to 10pm, are you flexible to work between these times?

**Camille:** I am.

**Heather:** Do you have to take off any time that you know of in the next 6 months?

**Camille:** Not that I know of.

**Heather:** All right and you are a certified trainer?

**Camille:** Yes, I am.

**Heather:** Okay, all right great and you are authorized to work in the United States?

**Camille:** Yes.

**Heather:** All right, so share with me what you know about our company here?

**Camille:** So, I know that you guys have been around for about 10 years, I recently started coming to your gym a year ago to take yoga classes and have loved it.

**Heather:** So describe your current job or your last job and responsibilities.

**Camille:** Okay. So I worked at a local gym, and I owned my own personal training company there.

**Heather:** Awesome.

**Camille:** Yeah, so I would work with clients usually in the mornings from about 6am to noon and help them reach their fitness goals.

**Heather:** Okay, great. So what is a major reason for you wanting to be a part of our team?

**Camille:** I think just seeing the family atmosphere and every time I come in I just feel like, I wanna stay here!

**Heather:** What skills have you acquired or built that you think you can bring to our team?

**Camille:** Yeah, well as I mentioned I am a certified personal trainer, I am currently taking a yoga certification course.

**Heather:** Where do you see yourself careerwise in the next 5 years?

**Camille:** I know you guys are looking to expand and open up other branches and that is something I would love to partner with.

**Heather:** Okay, great, tell me about a time when you had to solve a problem, maybe a difficult client. What would you have done differently, what was the outcome?

**Camille:** So I had a client, I was working with him for several months, he was awesome, but he got behind on his payments, about $400 behind and so I started to think like I can't keep working with him, but now we are kind of friends because we have been working together for months, but I had to just tell him, look I need you to get caught up on your payments before we can do any future personal training sessions together.

**Heather:** Okay, great. Well Camille I think that you would be a great fit to our team. You have the experience. You seem to genuinely have a passion for fitness. We do have a few other candidates but I definitely will be back in touch with you. Thanks for coming in.

**Camille:** Thank you so much for this opportunity.

# DIALOGUE 53
# Online Chatting

**James:** Hi. My name is James, it's nice to meet you.

**River:** Hey. I'm River. Where are you from?

**James:** I was born in America, but I'm working in Austria now. What about you?

**River:** Oh wow. I was born in England and I am still in England.

**James:** Nice. What do you do for work?

**River:** I'm a freelance wedding photographer. Most of the weddings I shoot are here in England, but I fly to Italy and Portugal for summer weddings.

**James:** That's fantastic. I'm a mechanical engineer. So tell me about your hobbies.

**River:** I like to swim, cook, and build model airplanes. I know it's random, but my dad got me into it when I was little, and I still enjoy it.

**James:** That's a fun hobby.

**River:** What about you?

**James:** I enjoy jogging, studying languages, and traveling.

**River:** Oh yeah? What languages do you speak?

**James:** I learned Spanish from my mom who was born in Spain. Then I took French in high school. Since transferring to Austria, I've been learning German.

**River:** Wow, that's really impressive. I've always said I should learn Italian or Portuguese because of my clients, but I'm so intimidated.

**James:** It's really not so hard. It just takes discipline, a little bit every day. But nowadays there are so many online resources.

**Rivers:** That's true. You've inspired me James. I have to go eat dinner now, but I hope we can chat again soon.

**James:** That would be nice.

## DIALOGUE 54

# Joining a Gym

**Trainer:** Hi, what brings you in today?

**Molly:** Hey. I'm looking to join your gym. Could you tell the price and services you offer?

**Trainer:** Sure. So our monthly membership is $39.99. Normally there is a one time fee to sign up, but we are running a special, so there will be no sign up fee. We also offer personal training and we have a pool. Both of those have an additional cost.

**Molly:** How many months do I have to commit to?

**Trainer:** It's month by month. So if you decide to leave after a month, no problem.

**Molly:** How much is the pool? What about the trainers?

**Trainer:** The pool is an extra $20 per month. The training packages vary. For one single session, it's $40. However, if you buy 10 sessions, the fee goes down to $25 per session.

**Molly:** Can I just pay for the training sessions or do I have to be a member of the gym?

**Trainer:** You have to be a member of the gym.

**Molly:** What group classes do you have?

**Trainer:** We have zumba, pilates, yoga, body pump, and a traditional aerobics class.

**Molly:** Wow, and those are all included in the gym membership?

**Trainer:** Yes they are. Our group classes are quite popular.

**Molly:** Okay, sign me up.

**Trainer:** Great. I'm just going to have you fill out some paperwork.

# DIALOGUE 55

# Tourists

**Tourism Office:** Hi. Feel free to take any brochures that you find interesting. If you have any questions, let me know.

**Larry:** Well it's my first time in New York. I want to see the Statue of Liberty, the Empire State Building, and Central Park. What else would you recommend?

**Tourism Office:** You've chosen some great sights. I would also recommend Rockefeller Center. The ice rink is closed in the summer but you can catch a great view from the top.

**Larry:** Oh that sounds wonderful.

**Tourism Office:** There are many amazing museums like the Metropolitan Museum of Art and the American Museum of Natural History.

**Larry:** My friends told me to go to a Broadway show.

**Tourism Office:** You know, if you can, I would recommend it. Shopping is a must too, 5th Avenue.

**Larry:** So much to do and see! I'm only here for 5 days.

**Tourism Office:** You can do a lot in 5 days. A new attraction that not so many people know about is called the High Line. It's a former rail line that's been transformed into an urban walking trail. I really recommend you to check it out. There are some amazing views.

**Larry:** Wow, I'm writing a list.

**Tourism Office:** Don't forget to see Brooklyn Bridge and the Trade Towers Memorial.

**Larry:** I hope I can fit it all in. Eating good food is a must too.

**Tourism Office:** Oh, you won't be disappointed. Here, take this brochure. It's for food lovers. It has the top 50 restaurants in the city, plus there are some discount coupons.

**Larry:** This is fantastic. I better get out there and explore!

**Tourism Office:** Have a great time.

# First Date

**Jax:** Wow, Judy, you look so beautiful tonight.

**Judy:** Oh thank you. This restaurant has such an amazing view. I didn't even know it existed.

**Jax:** Yeah, it's pretty sweet to see all the city lights. I've only been here once, but the food was amazing.

**Judy:** Do you remember what you ordered?

**Jax:** I had gotten a steak the last time, with these amazing garlic mashed potatoes.

**Judy:** Oh yum. I was looking at the mahi mahi. It sounds delicious.

**Jax:** Just be sure to save room for dessert. What is it you do for work again?

**Judy:** I'm a professor at a university. I teach in the arts department.

**Jax:** Oh very interesting. Are you an artist?

**Judy:** I guess you could say that. I'm an oil painter and a sculptor.

**Jax:** I would love to see your work sometime.

**Judy:** Sure, what is it that you do?

**Jax:** I'm a high school football coach. I had a college injury myself, so I could never make it pro, but I love the game and I love coaching.

**Judy:** Oh that's sweet. I'm sorry about your injury.

**Jax:** It's been a few years, so I'm used to it. I'm thankful I can still work out and enjoy my life.

**Judy:** I hear ya. Our health is such a gift. So shall we order?

**Jax:** Yes, you first.

# Photo Session

**Photographer:** I like the location you chose. The flowers are so beautiful here. Are we doing any outfit changes?

**Jasmine:** Thanks, yeah, it sure is a beautiful day. I have just this one dress.

**Photographer:** This is your first baby? How far along are you?

**Jasmine:** Yes. I'm 38 weeks. We're having a girl.

**Photographer:** That's amazing. Do you have a name yet?

**Jasmine:** Rose. I wanted to stick with a flower name, like mine. Plus my mom's name is Rose.

**Photographer:** I love it. Okay, so let's start with just you, standing, and then after we will pull in your husband okay?

**Jasmine:** Great. I'm starting to sweat already.

**Photographer:** Don't worry. You look gorgeous. Okay. If you can frame your tummy by making a heart over it with your hands that would be great.

**Jasmine:** Like this?

**Photographer:** Exactly. Perfect. Now look down at your belly. Great. Now, Logan, go in from behind and wrap your arms around her. Yes, oh this is adorable.

**Jasmine:** Can we take some photos sitting too? I brought this adorable picnic blanket.

**Photographer:** Of course! This is your session. We can do whatever you want.

**Jasmine:** Okay, Logan, can you set up the blanket?

**Photographer:** Okay, let's sit side by side and then I will have Logan go behind you like we did standing.

**Jasmine:** Okay. Let's do some looking at each other and a few kissing ones too.

**Photographer:** Cute! Yes, these are turning out great. Adorable. Okay, how about let's take some photos of you guys walking to finish the session?

**Jasmine:** That sounds great. I can't wait to see the final results.

**Photographer:** I will have them edited by the end of the week. **65**

DIALOGUE 58

# Upcoming Political Elections

**Rose:** This is my first time voting. I'm so excited.

**Dad:** The privileges of turning 18. Do you know who you're going to vote for?

**Rose:** I'm not sure. I've been learning a lot in my political science class.

**Dad:** You seem more interested in politics than before.

**Rose:** I know. The idea is intriguing to me. Maybe I'll run for class president.

**Dad:** Wow. Well you have my support if you do. You would need help with your campaign.

**Rose:** Yeah, it's a lot to process. So should we go vote together?

**Dad:** Yup. It's just a 5 minute walk from our house. It's all automated. You just need to bring your driver's license.

**Rose:** Do you think there will be a line?

**Dad:** Hopefully we missed the rush. So you know you can vote straight republican or democrat for everything or you can go through each candidate individually.

**Rose:** What do you mean? I thought this was just for the presidential elections.

**Dad:** It's everything dear, senate, house, the local elections too, like our sheriff.

**Rose:** Wow. I haven't looked into everything to know what they stand for.

**Dad:** I should have prepared you before. Your vote matters.

**Rose:** Next time, I'll be a lot more prepared. Who knows, maybe I'll even be the class president!

## DIALOGUE 59

# Running Club

**Tim:** Why did I let you convince me to be a part of this running club? I'm exhausted.

**Jill:** You're in the best shape of your life. Plus, it's only twice a week.

**Tim:** True, but it kills me every time.

**Jill:** No pain, no gain. We have our half marathon in three weeks. We need this training.

**Tim:** I still can't believe it. Six months ago, I had never ran more than 3 miles. Now I'm about to run 13.

**Jill:** It's amazing what consistent training does.

**Tim:** I'm a little nervous because my left knee sometimes bothers me.

**Jill:** You need to make sure to ice it after every run. At least you're wearing that supportive brace when you run. That should help.

**Tim:** I'm also stretching as much as I can.

**Jill:** That's good. You can also take anti-inflammatory medicine.

**Tim:** True. I need to remember that.

**Jill:** Well, have a good one. I gotta get home to take a shower before work. See you on Saturday.

**Tim:** Okay. After Saturday's run, we're going to get smoothies right?

**Jill:** Yes! I can't wait to check out that new smoothie bar on the West end of town. It looks adorable.

**Tim:** Great! Enjoy your day.

**Jill:** You too.

# Renting an Apartment

**Apartment manager:** What brings you in today?

**Tessa:** I have a friend who lives in this apartment complex and she loves it, especially the gym and pool.

**Apartment manager:** Those sure do draw people in. I have 2 apartments available for rent. One is a 1 bedroom and the other is a 2 bedroom.

**Tessa:** It's just me, so a one bedroom is fine.

**Apartment manager:** It's pretty big, just under 1100 square feet. It has a living room, kitchen, bathroom, and a small laundry room. It comes with a parking spot and as you know, a shared pool and gym.

**Tessa:** How much is the rent?

**Apartment manager:** It's $900 a month and we do require one month up front and a 12 month lease. There is also a $500 security deposit.

**Tessa:** How soon could I move in?

**Apartment manager:** You could move in tomorrow if you would like.

**Tessa:** And the apartment is furnished or unfurnished?

**Apartment manager:** Unfurnished.

**Tessa:** Okay. Let me get back to you. Thanks so much for the information.

**Apartment manager:** No problem. If I were you, I wouldn't wait too long. These apartments get snatched up quickly.

**Tessa:** Okay, I'll keep that in mind.

## DIALOGUE 61

# Renting a Car

**Rental agent:** What can I do for you today?

**Reese:** I just landed and I need a car for next week.

**Rental agent:** Okay. What size car are you looking for?

**Reese:** Something compact is fine. It's just for me.

**Rental agent:** Okay. Let me see. We have a Tesla available, a Ford Focus, or a Saturn.

**Reese:** How much is the Tesla?

**Rental agent:** We're looking at $1,100 for the week.

**Reese:** Ouch. And the others?

**Rental agent:** Remember you'll need to pay for fuel in the others. But both run at $540 for the week.

**Reese:** I'll take the Ford focus. I don't need anything too fancy.

**Rental agent:** Can I see your driver's license?

**Reese:** There you go.

**Rental agent:** Do you want to purchase insurance for the week?

**Reese:** No, my credit card covers car rentals.

**Rental agent:** Okay then. After taxes that will be $590. How would you like to pay?

**Reese:** Here is my visa.

**Rental agent:** Okay. Sign the rental agreement here and here.

**Reese:** Sure thing.

**Rental agent:** Okay, here is your receipt and a copy of the contract. Here are the keys and your car is parked in lot A number 44. Be sure to fill it up with gas before you return the car or you will be charged. Do you have any other questions?

**Reese:** Nope. I think you covered it. Thanks.

**Rental agent:** Thank you, and enjoy your stay in L.A.

# In the Courtroom

**Judge:** So do you declare to tell the whole truth and nothing but the truth?

**Scott:** Yes, I do.

**Judge:** You may proceed. What did you see on the night of Saturday May 15th?

**Scott:** I had just pumped gas. I was thirsty so I went into the convenience store to get some water. I was in front of the water section when all of a sudden I heard a man shout. "Get down, nobody move, I have a gun".

**Judge:** Continue your statement.

**Scott:** I was terrified. I wasn't sure if he saw me, so I got down low and dialed 911. He then told the cashier to give him all the money. I didn't have a clear view of the register. I was scared to move. When 911 picked up, I whispered my location and said "robbery".

**Judge:** At this time was there anyone else in the store?

**Scott:** There was one other man on the ground like me. He was so scared. Anyways, I am assuming the cashier gave the money, because I never heard a gunshot. I started to hear sirens in the distance.

**Judge:** Had you moved from your spot? Can you identify anything about the robber?

**Scott:** I could see he had black hair and a black hoodie with a skull on the back of it. That's it.

**Judge:** Is there anything else you want to say?

**Scott:** I think the man was working alone and he left on a blue bicycle. The cashier started to sob, so that's when I got up off the floor and I saw the man escaping on the bike. That's all I remember.

**Judge:** Thank you so much for your testimony. You may get down from the witness stand.

# Building a Puzzle with the Kids

**Mom:** Wow, what a cool puzzle grandma bought you. It has all 50 states. Let's dump out all the pieces.

**Maddox:** Yeah, I love this puzzle. I've done it like a million times.

**Mom:** Well since you're the expert, I can let you do it alone.

**Maddox:** Nah, it's more fun together. Let's put together the edges first.

**Mom:** Okay, oh here is California.

**Maddox:** I have Florida and Texas.

**Mom:** Do you think this puzzle is too easy for you?

**Maddox:** No, but maybe when I'm 10 it will be.

**Mom:** Oh man, this one doesn't fit. Oh it's upside down, that's why. There we go.

**Maddox:** I love Hawaii, I want to move back there. I miss the beach.

**Mom:** Someday we'll live by the ocean, probably not in Hawaii though.

**Maddox:** Where's New York? Why can't I find it?

**Mom:** There it is, it was buried under South Dakota and Nebraska.

**Maddox:** Does anyone even live in Nebraska?

**Mom:** Of course. I think there are a lot of farmers there.

**Maddox:** Here, I have Montana, and oh there's Georgia.

**Mom:** We're all over the place, but it's coming together.

**Maddox:** Yeah, I know. I love puzzles. Maybe we should buy one with all the countries in the world.

**Mom:** I can look online today. You know how much I love to travel.

## DIALOGUE 64
# The Kids Take a Bath

**Dad:** Ivory, Kairo, the bath is ready.

**Ivory:** Can we have bubbles?

**Dad:** Yes, but let me pour them in. You always waste them.

**Ivory:** Fine.

**Kairo:** Can we have a bath bomb?

**Dad:** Let's just stick with the bubbles.

**Ivory:** Kairo let's put all our toys in.

**Kairo:** Okay.

**Dad:** Let me wash your hair. There we go, let's rinse the soap out.

**Ivory:** So many bubbles.

**Dad:** Those are called suds.

**Ivory:** I want to wash my own body.

**Dad:** You can. Let me get you the soap.

**Ivory:** The bath is filling up dad.

**Dad:** I will turn off the water. Be careful not to pull the drain plug or all the water will go out.

**Kairo:** We will dad.

**Dad:** Have fun playing. Let me know when you're done. I'll get your towels and pajamas ready.

# Picking the Kids up from School

**Mom:** How was your day, kids?

**Maddox:** I'm happy it's Friday. We had gym today, so that was fun.

**Ivory:** And I had art class. Look at this picture that I drew.

**Mom:** Oh, that's beautiful honey. You're becoming quite the little artist.

**Maddox:** Can we stop and get ice cream? I'm hungry.

**Mom:** Actually we're meeting your cousin at the park.

**Maddox:** Oh yay, but mom, I'm so hungry.

**Mom:** I brought some snacks for you guys. Don't worry. You can eat them when we get to the park.

**Ivory:** I'm hungry too.

**Mom:** Don't worry guys, you can eat soon. Oh Maddox, your teacher sent home a note that next week is show and tell. What do you want to bring?

**Maddox:** I want to bring some legos that I built.

**Mom:** That's cool. Ivory, your teacher said that you are going on a field trip to the zoo.

**Ivory:** Yeah, I know mom.

**Mom:** Well, you both have things to look forward to next week.

# DIALOGUE 66

# Trying on Clothes

**Jocelyn:** I dunno, do you think I need a smaller size? It's kind of baggy in the stomach area.

**Jess:** I mean I can get you one if you want, but I don't love the pattern. Why don't you try on the other shirts?

**Jocelyn:** Okay, you're right. In the meantime, can you go browse the dresses? That's the real reason I came here, not for shirts.

**Jess:** Yeah, you said you wanted an elegant one right? Any certain color?

**Jocelyn:** I'm looking for something blue or red. I think those colors flatter me the most.

**Jess:** Long or short? Silk or cotton?

**Jocelyn:** The length isn't important. I would prefer something more dressy. It's for a dinner party.

**Jess:** And your price range?

**Jocelyn:** Under $150. Preferably under $100, but it's hard to find a good dress for under that price these days.

**Jess:** True. I'll go see if anything catches my eye.

**Jocelyn:** I'm going to try on these few shirts and jeans I have, then I'll be right out.

**Jess:** Oh, do you need any accessories? There is the cutest new boutique that just opened up and I've been dying to go.

**Jocelyn:** I guess it depends on the dress. I may also need some new shoes to go with it. But we can always run in there if you want.

**Jess:** Okay. Let's try to find you that dress sister!

# DIALOGUE 67

## At the Bank

**Bank teller:** Hi, what can I do for you today?

**Zac:** Hey. I need to deposit these checks.

**Bank teller:** Okay, can you fill out this deposit slip?

**Zac:** Sure. Oh I actually don't remember my account number.

**Bank teller:** Do you have your driver's license? I can look it up for you.

**Zac:** That, I do have.

**Bank teller:** Great. I have your account number. Can you hand me the slip? I can finish filling it out for you.

**Zac:** Oh that's so nice. Thanks.

**Bank teller:** Okay, so I am depositing $873 into your checking account. Is there anything else I can do for you today?

**Zac:** Actually, yes. I am looking to see if I can get pre-approved for a bank loan. I'm looking to buy a house.

**Bank teller:** I can't help you with that, but Thomas is in his office. He handles the loans. Let me call him and see if he's free.

**Zac:** Perfect.

**Bank teller:** So Thomas has an appointment now but if you would like to wait in our lobby for 30 minutes, he would be happy to see you.

**Zac:** I don't think I have the time. What about tomorrow?

**Bank teller:** Let me check. Yes, tomorrow you can come back at 10am. Does that work?

**Zac:** It sure does. I'll see you then.

**Bank teller:** Have a great afternoon.

**Zac:** You too.

# Under Arrest

**Christopher:** I don't understand why I'm being arrested. I did nothing wrong.

**Police:** Apparently there is a warrant out for your arrest.

**Christopher:** That's impossible. I didn't do anything.

**Police:** I'm seeing here that you have a bench warrant.

**Christopher:** I don't even know what that means.

**Police:** It means that you missed a mandated court appearance.

**Christopher:** I was never supposed to go to court.

**Police:** It says here that you were supposed to go in for jury duty.

**Christopher:** I never even knew about it.

**Police:** There's really nothing I can do.

**Christopher:** I want to talk to a lawyer. This is ridiculous.

**Police:** Anything you say can and will be used against you in a court of law.

**Christopher:** I'm appalled. Don't I at least get a phone call?

**Police:** Yes, you can make one call.

# How was Your Day?

**Wife:** Hey honey, how was your day?

**Husband:** Tiring. But we are making progress on the Jones' case. So that's good.

**Wife:** That's great news. I ordered Thai food for dinner. It should be here any minute.

**Husband:** Panang curry?

**Wife:** Your favorite. I also got pad thai and thai fried rice for the kids.

**Husband:** You're the best. How was your day?

**Wife:** Pretty good. The kids were a little rambunctious after school, but I did manage to get the house cleaned and I worked on my book for about an hour.

**Husband:** It is looking clean in here. Remember, I told you we can hire a weekly housekeeper to help lighten your load.

**Wife:** I know. And I appreciate that. I just can't justify paying $100 a week when I can do it myself.

**Husband:** Yeah, but your time is valuable too. Remember that?

**Wife:** Yeah, I know. Thanks for your support babe.

**Husband:** Of course. Kids! Thai food is here, come and eat!!

**Wife:** It smells amazing!

# What's the Weather Like?

**Emma:** It's so nice to hear from you too. How's Arizona? What's the weather like?

**Noah:** It's hot. But the climate is dry, so it's not so intense.

**Emma:** Oh yeah. It's so humid these days here in South Carolina.

**Noah:** I hear ya. But it's summer. You're in the rainy season right?

**Emma:** Well, normally we have afternoon thunderstorms but honestly, it's sunny every day.

**Noah:** I love sunshine. I'm in a better mood when it's sunny out.

**Emma:** Me too. But it is cozy with the rain too. I love to curl up with a good book and a cup of tea.

**Noah:** That's so cliche.

**Emma:** Maybe so, but it's the truth.

**Noah:** So when are you going to come out to visit me?

**Emma:** Maybe when the weather cools off. When is that?

**Noah:** Maybe October.

**Emma:** I have a school break over Thanksgiving. Will you be there?

**Noah:** I should be.

**Emma:** I'll plan to come then. I don't want to miss Christmas with my family. It's my favorite time of the year.

**Noah:** But it's cold, and sometimes snowy.

**Emma:** True, but it doesn't last long.

**Noah:** Yeah you're right. It's short lived.

# On a Hike

**Jana:** What a gorgeous day.

**Cliff:** It really is. I'm so glad we decided to go on this hike.

**Jana:** It's what, 6 miles round trip?

**Cliff:** About that. Most people say they spend about 3 hours total, because the view at the top is so stunning.

**Jana:** I can't wait. I'm going to put on some bug spray and sunblock. Want any?

**Cliff:** Sure. I packed some sandwiches, apples, granola, and water in my backpack.

**Jana:** I also threw some chips in there.

**Cliff:** I didn't even notice. Are you ready to get started?

**Jana:** I am, I think the first part is fairly flat with a lot of little creeks and streams.

**Cliff:** They said we might even see some deer.

**Jana:** Oh, I think there is also a small waterfall towards the end.

**Cliff:** Oh shoot, I meant to bring my hiking stick. I must have left it in the garage.

**Jana:** I'm sure you'll find one on the trail that you can use.

**Cliff:** Yeah, maybe. It's not absolutely necessary, but it does help me. My knees are a little weak.

**Jana:** Well here then, take mine. I don't really need it.

**Cliff:** Thanks. Wow, it's already starting to get hot. I'm so glad we got started early.

**Jana:** The early bird gets the worm. I also like coming early because there aren't as many people.

**Cliff:** It's like we have the whole place to ourselves.

**Jana:** Exactly, now let's go!

# Crossing the Street

**Rylee:** Be careful son, do you see the red light? That means we have to stop.

**Dax:** Yeah, I see it mom. When it's green we can go.

**Rylee:** Exactly. Can you press the button? That way when the light turns green we can walk.

**Dax:** Sure.

**Rylee:** This is called a crosswalk. Because it's for us to walk across.

**Dax:** And we're pedestrians.

**Rylee:** How did you learn such a big word?

**Dax:** They taught us in school.

**Rylee:** You're smart. Oh the light turned green. But still look both ways.

**Dax:** No cars are coming. Let's go. Oh, it's counting down.

**Rylee:** Yes we still have 20 seconds to cross the street.

**Dax:** Should we run?

**Rylee:** No, we'll be able to get across in time. Don't worry.

**Dax:** Oh yeah. You're right. We still have ten seconds to spare.

**Rylee:** Told ya so.

## DIALOGUE 73

# At the Mechanic

**Mechanic:** What seems to be the problem?

**Jasper:** I have no idea. The check engine light came on yesterday. Everything seems to be fine.

**Mechanic:** Okay, I can run some tests and see what I find. What year is the car?

**Jasper:** It's a 2016.

**Mechanic:** If you can stick around for 30 minutes, I should have some news for you.

**Jasper:** I can do that. Do you have a bathroom I can use?

**Mechanic:** Around the corner to the right. Feel free.

**Jasper:** Thanks.

**Mechanic:** So I have some good news for you. You're overdue for an oil change and your spark plugs are pretty dirty. I can change your oil and the spark plugs for just $64. Do you want me to do that?

**Jasper:** Yes. Oh good. I was afraid it was something serious.

**Mechanic:** Nope, nothing serious came up when I ran the diagnostics.

**Jasper:** Well great. I'll just wait in the lobby while you change the oil then.

**Mechanic:** Perfect. I'll come get you when I finish.

**Jasper:** I appreciate it.

# DIALOGUE 74
# Visiting a Sick Friend

**Theresa:** Oh the flowers are so beautiful. You didn't have to do that.

**Joyce:** Oh it's nothing. I hoped to brighten your day.

**Theresa:** I appreciate you coming. This chemo treatment is rough. I'm so tired.

**Joyce:** But you're on your last round right?

**Theresa:** I have one more after this one. Fingers crossed to finally be cancer free.

**Joyce:** You're a fighter Theresa! You will beat this. I have faith.

**Theresa:** You've been such a good friend through this all. I would never wish this upon anyone, but you see who your true friends are when you go through something like this.

**Joyce:** I wish I could do more. Sometimes I feel so helpless.

**Theresa:** You visiting me here in the hospital, messaging me, praying for me, it means so much.

**Joyce:** It's the least I can do really. Are you hungry? I brought you your favorite soup.

**Theresa:** I actually am a little hungry. Thank you.

**Joyce:** Is there anything else I can get for you? I can spend about 20 more minutes before I have to get back to work.

**Theresa:** If you wouldn't mind listening to some music with me over lunch, that would be nice.

**Joyce:** I would be happy to. Hillsong again?

**Theresa:** Yes, it really touches my soul every time I listen to it.

**Joyce:** It is beautiful.

## DIALOGUE 75

# Paying for Parking

**Miranda:** I'm so confused. I miss old-fashioned parking when you just paid a person.

**Edward:** I know, now we have to pay a box.

**Miranda:** But how does it work? Do you get it?

**Edward:** Let me see. Yeah, so you just put in your parking number spot and then you have to pay with a visa. This machine doesn't accept cash.

**Miranda:** Okay. I'm in number A3.

**Edward:** Let me pay this time. You drove.

**Miranda:** Oh thanks! You're kind.

**Edward:** Okay, see, I put in my visa. It says the rate is $2.00 per hour.

**Miranda:** Oh, it's cheaper than I expected.

**Edward:** That wasn't too bad was it?

**Miranda:** No it wasn't. But sometimes I miss human contact. It seems like everything is going to machines and done electronically. Just think of how many people are out of jobs.

**Edward:** I understand where you're coming from.

**Miranda:** So it's Japanese or Vietnamese food tonight? I'm torn.

**Edward:** How about Vietnamese? I am in the mood for Pho.

**Miranda:** Works for me!

## DIALOGUE 76
# Should We Have Kids?

**Matt:** Yeah, but our lives will change forever.

**Patricia:** But it could be a good thing. We're already 30. If we're going to do this, we really have to try now.

**Matt:** Imagine, no more trips on a whim, gone are the days where we sleep through the night.

**Patricia:** Yeah, but there are benefits too.

**Matt:** I mean, I know it's a unique opportunity to create little humans. I'm just not sure it's for us.

**Patricia:** Are you afraid?

**Matt:** I don't think I'm afraid. I'm just not sure it's for us. We like our freedom. We can spend our money on things like travel and concerts instead of kids.

**Patricia:** But just imagine a mini Matti running around the house. You could teach him so many things. It would be adorable.

**Matt:** I have my nephews for that. I enjoy having them over but I'm always so happy when they leave. I like to have my space.

**Patricia:** What if we just try for six months. No baby, then it's meant to be.

**Matt:** I don't know if I can commit to that. What if we get pregnant right away?

**Patricia:** Then it means it's meant to be. Come on, we would be great parents.

**Matt:** Let's sleep on it.

## DIALOGUE 77
# Buying or Renting a House?

**Haley:** I don't know. The housing market is so hot right now. Does it make sense to buy when houses are so expensive?

**Brandon:** I mean the prices could just increase even more next year.

**Haley:** What if we rented for a year and see if prices go down?

**Brandon:** Well then that means paying at least $1200 a month in rent for the next year. That could be part of our down payment. Plus there is no guarantee that the housing prices will go down.

**Haley:** It's so hard to know what to do. Obviously I don't want to throw money away.

**Brandon:** I think we should commit to looking to buy a house for the next three months. We know our budget is max $300,000, if we don't find anything, then let's rent.

**Haley:** Okay. Gosh, this feels stressful, but house shopping should be fun.

**Brandon:** In a market like this we have to move fast. We have to be willing to make an offer the day the house goes on the market because so many houses are literally selling in a day.

**Haley:** Gosh. Okay. I just need to change my perspective and think more positively. I'm willing to do this.

**Brandon:** I'm already on the phone with a realtor.

**Haley:** I'm going to check some sites online, just to see if anything catches my eye.

**Brandon:** Good idea.

# DIALOGUE 78

# Buying a Car

**Silas:** It's my first car dad. I have to have something reliable.

**Dad:** Reliable, I agree. But I'm not paying $30,000 for a new car. You're 16 years old. It's your first car.

**Silas:** But think about how long it will last dad. I will take care of it.

**Dad:** Silas, I know you will, you're responsible, but it's too expensive. We need to find something that costs less than $20,000.

**Silas:** Oh man, I was really looking forward to that new car.

**Dad:** I know it has all the bells and whistles, but it's not necessary at your age.

**Silas:** But Damien just got a brand new car.

**Dad:** So that's what this is really about? You're trying to compete with your friend?

**Silas:** No. Maybe. I dunno. I just don't want some old junker.

**Dad:** You're being a bit dramatic. I don't think it's possible to pay 20 grand for a junker.

**Silas:** Maybe you're right. I'm just being paranoid.

**Dad:** So, you want a manual car, preferably newer than 2015, a nice stereo system and preferably low mileage?

**Silas:** Yeah. I really like white and silver for colors.

**Dad:** Ok. Well, let's plan to go car shopping this Saturday together. Hopefully we can find something.

**Silas:** That would be great. Thanks dad. You're the best.

**Dad:** It's exciting to buy your first car. I'm happy to share this experience with you.

## DIALOGUE 79

# Adopting a Baby

**Melo:** I can't believe this is finally happening.

**Jed:** And so quickly too. I never expected that we would have a baby in three weeks time.

**Melo:** It's much faster than a pregnancy.

**Jed:** True, do you think we can get her room ready in time?

**Melo:** Yes, my mom and sisters are coming over this weekend. We will do a room makeover. It will be ready this weekend. You know how my mom is.

**Jed:** Amazing. Do you need anything else?

**Melo:** Since this is our 3rd kid, I have most things. Maybe just some clothes.

**Jed:** Are your sisters going to throw you a baby shower?

**Melo:** I think so. But I want to keep it small. Just a few friends and family.

**Jed:** That's a good idea. Wow. It's still so surreal.

**Melo:** I know. Are you ready for interrupted sleep again?

**Jed:** Not so much, but to have a girl will be worth it.

**Melo:** Your princess, finally.

**Jed:** I already have one princess. Now I'll have another.

**Melo:** You're so sweet. Should we go celebrate by having dinner out tonight?

**Jed:** You read my mind!

# Making a Smoothie

**Bryan:** I'm excited to finally try your famous smoothie.

**Camille:** It's going to change your life, trust me.

**Bryan:** So what's it in?

**Camille:** Spinach, kale, and mint.

**Bryan:** That's it?

**Camille:** Don't get ahead of the game. Strawberries, pineapple, and coconut water.

**Bryan:** It sounds refreshing, but I'm a little scared to try all those greens.

**Camille:** Come on, you love working out and eating.

**Bryan:** I like meat.

**Camille:** Haha true. But just have an open mind.

**Bryan:** What else do you need me to get from the freezer?

**Camille:** Just the strawberries.

**Bryan:** Okay, here you go.

**Camille:** Okay, so let's just add all the ingredients to the blender.

**Bryan:** Your blender is massive.

**Camille:** I know. It's a Vitamix. It's amazing.

**Bryan:** Wow, you're right. This smoothie seems like one you would find in a smoothie shop, no chunks.

**Camille:** I know right? Now try it. Be honest. What do you think?

**Bryan:** Wow. I'm impressed. It's better than I thought it would be.

**Camille:** I told you to trust me.

**Bryan:** You never let me down.

# Using a Computer

**Peter:** You need to open google drive. It's under the shared folder tab.

**Adrian:** But I'm not seeing the icon.

**Peter:** It's not an icon. You have to go to the website.

**Adrian:** Oh gosh. I'm not tech savvy at all.

**Peter:** There is a learning curve.

**Adrian:** I thought maybe it was just something for a MAC.

**Peter:** Nope, anyone can access google drive. Do you see it?

**Adrian:** Yes.

**Peter:** Okay, so open the video that I sent you and then save it to your computer. After that you can send it to your phone because I know you prefer to edit on there.

**Adrian:** It's true. It's so much easier to use than a computer.

**Peter:** Do you need help with anything else?

**Adrian:** Do you offer computer classes?

**Peter:** Haha no, but there are a lot of free tutorials on youtube. You know what youtube is right?

**Adrian:** Haha, very funny.

**Peter:** I couldn't resist teasing you.

**Adrian:** It's okay. I saw it coming. I'll let you know if I need anything else. Thanks so much for your help.

**Peter:** Anytime.

# Lost Keys

**Dane:** Have you seen my keys? I can't seem to find them.

**Darci:** That's why we have the little basket on the entrance table. It's for your keys.

**Dane:** I know. I'm not used to it yet.

**Darci:** Have you checked all your pockets?

**Dane:** Yeah, I even checked in between the couch cushions.

**Darci:** We waste so much of our time looking for things.

**Dane:** If my head wasn't attached to my body, I would lose it.

**Darci:** Oh, you were out in your shop. Did you leave the keys out there?

**Dane:** I'll go check.

**Darci:** I'll go look around the house.

**Dane:** Any luck?

**Darci:** Nope. This is getting annoying.

**Dane:** I'm already late for work.

**Darci:** Maybe you left them in your truck.

**Dane:** You'll never believe it. They were still in the ignition.

**Darci:** Oh my gosh. Well I hope you have a good day at work.

**Dane:** Thanks for helping me look.

# Car Accident

**Isaiah:** Are you okay?

**Titan:** Yeah man, just a little shocked.

**Isaiah:** We just got rear ended.

**Titan:** They hit us hard enough for the airbags to go off.

**Isaiah:** I'm just glad no one got hurt.

**Titan:** Your bumper got destroyed. And the front of their car.

**Isaiah:** It's a bummer for sure.

**Titan:** I think someone already called the police. We'll have to file a report.

**Isaiah:** I don't think we'll need a tow truck though. I'm going to call an auto body shop.

**Titan:** There's one not too far from here.

**Isaiah:** I think we're thinking of the same one. It's near my house.

**Titan:** I hate these fender benders. This is only the second one I've ever been in, but it's scary.

**Isaiah:** I know. Gets the adrenaline going.

**Titan:** For real. That car shouldn't have been tailgating us like that.

**Isaiah:** It's definitely going to be their fault. Their insurance should cover it.

**Titan:** Totally. I'm just glad no one got hurt.

**Isaiah:** Me too. We can count our blessings. It could have been much worse.

**Titan:** For real. Oh there's the police. Are you ready to talk to them?

**Isaiah:** Yeah. Let's go.

# Wedding Planning

**Maggie:** Thanks so much for helping me. I couldn't do this without you.

**Wedding planner:** It's my job. I'm happy to help.

**Maggie:** I'm so glad you were able to reserve the hotel. It's my favorite place.

**Wedding planner:** It's gorgeous. I'll call the catering company and the florist this week.

**Maggie:** I think we have finally chosen the band.

**Wedding planner:** That's great news. So have you registered yet for your bridal shower?

**Maggie:** I will do that on Saturday. The invitations also just arrived so I'm going to address those and send them out soon.

**Wedding planner:** Awesome. I've also confirmed your photographer and videographer.

**Maggie:** It's really all coming together!

**Wedding planner:** Yes, quite well. You've found your dress. Have you decided what to do for your rehearsal dinner?

**Maggie:** My fiance's parents are going to take care of that. We're going to our favorite restaurant.

**Wedding planner:** Okay, in two weeks I've scheduled a cake tasting. We're really making great progress.

**Maggie:** I know. I can't believe it. Just three more months until I marry the man of my dreams.

**Wedding planner:** Do you know where you're going on your honeymoon?

**Maggie:** We're going to spend 2 weeks in Greece. We've never been there before. I'm so excited.

**Wedding planner:** That sounds amazing. I'll touch base with you in a few days. Let me know if you need anything.

**Maggie:** Will do. Thanks again.

## DIALOGUE 85

# Getting a Divorce

**Ezra:** I just got my divorce papers from my attorney.

**Jack:** Wow man. I'm so sorry.

**Ezra:** It sucks for sure. We've already been separated for a year, but it's hitting me in a new way.

**Jack:** I'm sure. You guys were together for 8 years.

**Ezra:** We wanted to make it work. But at the end of the day, we're better off apart.

**Jack:** What really happened?

**Ezra:** We want different things in life. Her career is more important than having kids.

**Jack:** Wow. Well you're still young. You can still find someone and have a family.

**Ezra:** It's true. I think she has already signed the papers. So once I sign, the divorce settlement is final.

**Jack:** Was it complicated?

**Ezra:** Not really. We don't own a house together and we don't have any kids. We had a shared bank account so the money was split between the two of us.

**Jack:** How's Tia holding up? Have you talked to her?

**Ezra:** It's too painful. We haven't spoken in months.

**Jack:** I'm so sorry to hear that. You have my support.

**Ezra:** I appreciate that. Divorce is never easy.

# Negotiation

**Supply company:** Our rate is $1 per unit if you're purchasing over 100 units.

**Tamara:** I understand. But I'm looking to buy thousands of units. I need a better price.

**Supply company:** There's a possibility we can give you a better deal. Let me talk to my manager. Can you hold please?

**Tamara:** Sure.

**Supply company:** Okay. We can go to .90 per unit.

**Tamara:** That's not cutting it for me. I plan to be a long term client. I can pay .70 max.

**Supply company:** I'll have to talk to my manager again.

**Tamara:** Or I can do it.

**Supply company:** He's super busy. Please hold.

**Tamara:** Okay.

**Supply company:** Okay. Since you are a new customer we can only go as low as .80 per unit. However, my manager said that if you stay consistent and order for 3 months, we can go as low as .70 for future orders.

**Tamara:** It's a deal. I need to order 2000 units today.

**Supply company:** I will send over the paperwork. How are you going to pay?

**Tamara:** I will use a visa card.

**Supply company:** Okay. I will send over the agreement. Once you sign, there will be an option for you to pay by visa. What's your email address?

**Tamara:** tamara@samretail.com

**Supply company:** Okay. I'll get that right over to you. Thank you so much for your call. We look forward to working with you.

**Tamara:** Me too. I appreciate it.

# DIALOGUE 87
# The Diagnosis

**Doctor:** It's allergies. Your daughter is allergic to nuts and eggs, hence the reactions.

**Ally:** Oh my gosh. I had no idea. What a relief to finally have some answers.

**Doctor:** Yes. After running all the tests, this is what it comes down to. It can be challenging at first to cut eggs and nuts out of the diet but after time you will get used to it.

**Ally:** Can she ever be completely healed?

**Doctor:** Since she is only 2, there is a chance that she will outgrow this allergy. It's possible.

**Ally:** It's so strange because I don't have any food allergies, my husband either.

**Doctor:** I understand. Food allergies are quite common in kids. It's nothing to be alarmed about.

**Ally:** So is there anything else I can do?

**Doctor:** Obviously avoid eggs and nuts. When you go to restaurants, be sure to specify the food allergies to your server. If she has any more reactions, you will need to bring her to the ER. It can be very serious.

**Ally:** Okay. I'm still a bit shaken up. But so glad we have some answers. We have been running tests for the last two months.

**Doctor:** I know what you mean. Don't worry. You're a great mom, doing everything possible to take care of your baby.

**Ally:** Thank you. Thanks so much for your time.

**Doctor:** You're welcome. Take care now.

## DIALOGUE 88

# At the Dermatologist

**Dermatologist:** So there are two moles that I would like to remove on your neck. Other than that, anything else you would like to get done is up to you.

**Wendy:** Are they cancerous?

**Dermatologist:** In my opinion, no. We will send them to the lab to be tested. I'm removing them as a precaution.

**Wendy:** Ok, that's a relief.

**Dermatologist:** No worries. Is there anything else I can help you with today?

**Wendy:** Actually yes. I have this rash that breaks out on my stomach every once in a while. I have it now.

**Dermatologist:** Let me take a look.

**Wendy:** See?

**Dermatologist:** I do see. I think it's a breakout caused by sweat. Are you working out a lot?

**Wendy:** Yes. Actually I started a new workout plan last month. It's tough!

**Dermatologist:** So what I would recommend is actually changing your clothes! Make sure the fabric is breathable and try to shower right after you workout so that the sweat doesn't stay on your body.

**Wendy:** Oh my. Okay, I can do that. Who would have thought that sweat could cause such a problem?

**Dermatologist:** Haha, don't worry. I've seen crazier things.

**Wendy:** Well I appreciate your help.

**Dermatologist:** We will be giving you a call when we get your results back from the lab.

**Wendy:** I'll try not to worry.

**Dermatologist:** Good. You really shouldn't.

# Getting my Nails Done

**Nail tech:** What can I do for you today?

**Paige:** I would like to get my nails done.

**Nail tech:** Okay. Do you want a standard or spa manicure?

**Paige:** What's the difference?

**Nail tech:** Our standard manicure includes cutting the nails and the nail polish. It's $15. Our spa manicure also includes soaking the hands, massage and exfoliation. It's $25.

**Paige:** I think I will try the spa manicure. Can I do gel nail polish?

**Nail tech:** Sure. The price increases by $10 but it's worth it. You can choose a color of polish right over there.

**Paige:** I'm trying to decide between red and pink.

**Nail tech:** I think this blush color would look great with your skin tone.

**Paige:** I'll go with that then.

**Nail tech:** Great. Please take a seat in this chair and you can put your hands in the water.

**Paige:** How much time do you think this will take? I just realized I have another appointment in an hour.

**Nail tech:** Don't worry. I will be done in 40 minutes.

**Paige:** Okay great. I've already heard such great reviews about your place, I'm glad to finally come check it out myself.

**Nail tech:** Oh that's great. We're happy you came. You can also turn on the massage feature on the chair.

**Paige:** Oh this is going to be relaxing.

## DIALOGUE 90

# At the University

**Taylor:** I just can't decide. It's too hard.

**College counselor:** It's not easy. I recommend students to choose business as a major. Then if you decide you want to study something else, it won't be a hard transition.

**Taylor:** How many classes should I take per semester?

**College counselor:** To hold your football scholarship, you will have to take between 4-5 classes per semester.

**Taylor:** That feels like such an overload. How will I have time for football practice?

**College counselor:** You'd be surprised. All of our athletes take that many classes. It takes a lot of focus, but it's possible.

**Taylor:** So for the first semester, what classes should I take?

**College counselor:** All students have to take the prerequisite classes such as biology, math, English, history. I also strongly encourage you to take a foreign language class.

**Taylor:** My mom is Mexican, so I already speak Spanish.

**College counselor:** There is always German, Chinese, or French.

**Taylor:** I'll think about it. Learning a language is a lot of work. I guess you can go ahead and sign me up for the classes you first mentioned.

**College counselor:** I'm assuming you want morning classes since most athletes have practice in the afternoons?

**Taylor:** Yes. Exactly.

**College counselor:** Alright, well let's go ahead and get you enrolled.

## DIALOGUE 91

# Hobbies

**Kelly:** Oh, I never asked you about your hobbies.

**Jason:** What do you mean?

**Kelly:** What are they?

**Jason:** Oh. I love surfing, skating, and drawing.

**Kelly:** Wow, that's cool. I took a drawing class in college. It was pretty fun.

**Jason:** I love to draw people. What are your hobbies?

**Kelly:** I take a weekly dance class. I also enjoy reading and hiking.

**Jason:** There is this great surf spot, but you have to hike to get there. Maybe we should go sometime.

**Kelly:** That would be fun. I love the beach.

**Jason:** You also love to read. You can read while I surf.

**Kelly:** I also have a strange hobby. I love to fly kites. I know it's weird but I would go every week with my dad. I think it's more nostalgic than anything.

**Jason:** You can bring a kite if you want.

**Kelly:** I will do that. Should we go this weekend? It's supposed to be gorgeous.

**Jason:** Yes. Saturday works for me. The waves are better in the morning though. Is 7am too early for you?

**Kelly:** Eeek. A little but I can swing it. I can always take a nap on the beach.

**Jason:** Perfect. See you soon.

# DIALOGUE 92
## Stuck in the Elevator

**David:** Well this is unexpected.

**Janette:** I know. I've actually never been stuck in an elevator before.

**David:** Are you claustrophobic?

**Janette:** No, but I prefer to be out in the open!

**David:** I pressed the call button for help, but no one has responded yet.

**Janette:** Hopefully soon!

**David:** Oh there is someone. Yes, we are stuck in the elevator. No, the buttons don't work.

**Janette:** At least they are sending someone.

**David:** Yeah, for real!! Didn't you have an appointment in like 10 minutes?

**Janette:** Yes, I tried to message but I don't have any phone service in here.

**David:** Hopefully you can reschedule.

**Janette:** I hope. I waited a month for this appointment.

**David:** Oh I hear someone outside the elevator.

**Janette:** Finally.

**David:** Oh good. Thank you for helping us.

**Janette:** I'm going to call and see if I can arrive late to my appointment.

**David:** Good luck. I'll see you later.

**Janette:** Enjoy the rest of your day.

**David:** You too. Maybe take the stairs for the rest of the day!

# DIALOGUE 93
# City or Country Life

**Kristin:** I think the city is more practical.

**Jeff:** But we both work from home. It would be nice to have some land.

**Kristin:** But gas prices have really gone up. Can you imagine having to drive an hour just to get groceries?

**Jeff:** There are definitely some downsides.

**Kristin:** Plus there are several big parks in the city. There is even that new cafe overlooking the river. We can work from there for a change of scenery.

**Jeff:** True. But we don't have a backyard. I love outdoor space.

**Kristin:** But we have a huge terrace and our view overlooking the city is magical.

**Jeff:** I do love our location. It is convenient and the view is amazing, especially at night.

**Kristin:** How about we stay here for one more year and then revisit this discussion?

**Jeff:** Okay, you've convinced me. But I'm going to reserve an Airbnb next week in the country.

**Kristin:** As long as there is internet for work, I am down.

**Jeff:** Deal.

# DIALOGUE 94

# Encouragement

**Daisy:** I know you've been a little bummed since losing your job.

**Frank:** You can say that again.

**Daisy:** But Frank, it's been a month. You have to move forward.

**Frank:** I don't see any job opportunities around.

**Daisy:** You're so talented in so many areas Frank. You were the best in your company, there has to be something for you.

**Frank:** Oh thank you Daisy. That was kind.

**Daisy:** Plus you are young and vibrant. You're full of energy and creative. Why don't you start your own consulting firm?

**Frank:** Do you really think I could?

**Daisy:** Of course. You have all the skill sets, you're a likable guy, and you could even start from your home.

**Frank:** I don't know why I hadn't thought about this before.

**Daisy:** You've been so bummed about losing your job, you got lost in your own world.

**Frank:** Wow, you're right. Thanks for coming over here and encouraging me today. You may have changed my life.

**Daisy:** I don't know if I would go that far. But that's what friends are for.

**Frank:** Really, thank you. It means so much to me.

**Daisy:** I can't wait to watch you succeed!

# DIALOGUE 95
# Decorating the House

**Helen:** I was hoping to go for more of a bohemian, natural look in my bedroom.

**Interior designer:** Your walls are blue. How do you feel about going beige?

**Helen:** I like that idea.

**Interior designer:** I'm envisioning white bedding, but we could do some cool accent pillows and a throw blanket. I will stay with mostly neutral colors but also add some tones of yellow and orange.

**Helen:** What about this rug?

**Interior designer:** The rug is neutral, so it can stay. However, the light fixture, curtain, and paintings all need to go.

**Helen:** I imagined so. It's been about 10 years since I've decorated this room.

**Interior designer:** Some things are outdated, but some things still work.

**Helen:** What about that chair in the corner?

**Interior designer:** I think it can stay, but we should put a new pillow and throw blanket on it to freshen it up.

**Helen:** Realistically, how much money are we looking at to do all of this?

**Interior designer:** You had told me your budget was $5,000. Since we aren't making any large purchases, I think we can do this for under $4,000.

**Helen:** That's great. And the time frame?

**Interior designer:** By the end of the month, your new room will be ready.

**Helen:** I can't wait to see the results!

## DIALOGUE 96

# How did the Interview go?

**Iris:** So how did it go?

**Jacqueline:** Gosh. I'm not sure. I was so nervous at first.

**Iris:** I can imagine. But you're qualified for this job. You have experience.

**Jacqueline:** Yes. I know. But it's a manager position. It's a new level for me.

**Iris:** When do you think you will hear back from them?

**Jacqueline:** They said by the end of the week.

**Iris:** That's great. Well you did your best.

**Jacqueline:** But what if I don't get the job? I need this job.

**Iris:** Stay positive. Don't worry about what you can't control.

**Jacqueline:** You're right. I need to stay positive. If it doesn't work out, there has to be something better out there for me.

**Iris:** Yes. I think it'll work out. You're perfect for the job.

**Jacqueline:** You're such a good friend. Thanks for always believing in me.

**Iris:** Of course. I have your back!

**Jacqueline:** Wanna go grab dinner? I'm starving.

**Iris:** I'm so sorry, I already have dinner plans. But keep me in the loop ok?

**Jacqueline:** Okay. Maybe I'll just order take out.

## DIALOGUE 97

# Jet Lag

**Claudia:** Can we sleep yet? I'm exhausted.

**Damien:** Unfortunately no. It's only 4pm. If you sleep now, you'll wake up at 1 in the morning.

**Claudia:** I feel like I can't hold my eyes open for another minute.

**Damien:** Maybe we should go get dinner out.

**Claudia:** Maybe I need a shot of espresso or something to keep me awake.

**Damien:** Yeah, jet lag is no joke. But the best way to overcome it is by trying to stick to the schedule of the place you're in and by drinking a lot of water.

**Claudia:** True. I have dealt with jet lag before, but never like this.

**Damien:** Well there is a 12 hour time difference between New York and China. It's like night and day difference.

**Claudia:** Yeah. We already go on our first tour in two days.

**Damien:** I think we'll adjust fine. It's a mental game.

**Claudia:** If you say so. I think I am hungry. I'm so tired that my body doesn't know what it wants.

**Damien:** There is a noodle shop just a block away. Should we go?

**Claudia:** Okay. Let's go. Can you carry me?

# Yard Work

**Adelee:** Thanks for coming to help. My yard is so big, it would take me forever to do this alone.

**Lucas:** No problem. I'll focus on mowing the lawn and trimming the hedges.

**Adelee:** That would be amazing. I need to pull some weeds in the garden.

**Lucas:** You should also rake those leaves over there. There are so many that it could kill your grass.

**Adelee:** Do you think? Maybe I will rake first then.

**Lucas:** That's a good idea. Are you planning on planting these flowers too?

**Adelee:** Yes. I still haven't gotten around to it. Too much to do, too little time.

**Lucas:** One thing at a time.

**Adelee:** How much time do you have to help me today?

**Lucas:** The whole day. I think we can get everything done if we work all day.

**Adelee:** My dad is coming over after lunch to help me too.

**Lucas:** Oh that's awesome. Maybe he can plant the flowers.

**Adelee:** Maybe, he is bringing over some fresh mulch to put in the flower beds.

**Lucas:** Wow, your whole yard is going to get a makeover.

**Adelee:** I'm motivated because I'm having a party here next weekend. I want to have everything looking fresh.

**Lucas:** That's great. Well, let's get to work! The grass won't cut itself.

# DIALOGUE 99
# Buying a New Pet

**Abigail:** Can we get this one mommy? It's so cute!

**Mommy:** Oh I dunno honey. He's a puppy now, but he will get huge.

**Abigail:** Really? I want a doggy that will stay little forever.

**Mommy:** That's a good idea. Since we're in an apartment, I think we need something small.

**Abigail:** What about this one? He is so fluffy and white.

**Mommy:** What a cute little furball.

**Abigail:** So far he is my favorite.

**Mommy:** He is adorable and he will stay small.

**Abigail:** Can we pick out some new toys for him?

**Mommy:** Sure. We also need a bed for him, a collar, a leash, some dog food and a water dish.

**Abigail:** That's a lot of stuff.

**Mommy:** A dog is a big responsibility Abigail. You're going to have to take him out to go to the bathroom.

**Abigail:** I know. I am so happy to have him. I'll be responsible.

**Mommy:** Let's ask the store employee if he has had his shots. Then we can take him home.

**Abigail:** I'm so excited. I'm going to name him Leo.

# DIALOGUE 100
# Compliments

**Holly:** Girl, you are looking fine. I love your new dress.

**Tiara:** Oh, you're too sweet.

**Holly:** Seriously, where did you get your shoes? They are so cute!

**Tiara:** I bought both the shoes and dress in that little boutique downtown.

**Holly:** I still haven't been there.

**Tiara:** You should go. By the way, I adore your jacket. It's to die for!

**Holly:** Oh thank you. It's one of a kind. I designed it.

**Tiara:** You're kidding! I'm impressed. It's so chic.

**Holly:** Aww, that means a lot to me. I've been thinking about selling my clothes.

**Tiara:** You totally could. Your bag is super classy too. It goes perfectly with your jacket.

**Holly:** Thanks. I designed them together. I got so tired of looking for things that I envisioned in my mind that I decided to pull out my sewing machine and start making them myself.

**Tiara:** You are mega talented. I would love to check out your other designs.

**Holly:** You can come over this weekend if you want.

**Tiara:** Great! I will plan on it.

# Welcoming a New Neighbor

**Grace:** Hey, you're new right?

**Mckenzie:** Yeah. I just moved here from California.

**Grace:** Wow, that's on the other side of the country.

**Mckenzie:** It's work related, but honestly I'm happy for a change. California is so expensive and traffic is crazy.

**Grace:** It's a slower pace of life here in Georgia.

**Mckenzie:** I need that. I am honestly a little burnt out from the fast pace of life in California.

**Grace:** I understand. Can I offer you some sweet tea? It's pretty hot out today.

**Mckenzie:** You know, I've heard of sweet tea, but I've never tried it. Sure, I would love some.

**Grace:** I'll be right back. I'm Grace, by the way. I live just two doors down.

**Mckenzie:** Mckenzie. Nice to meet you. I appreciate you coming by.

**Grace:** This is a really friendly neighborhood. When I saw the moving truck in front of your house, I was curious!

**Mckenzie:** Well, I appreciate it. I never met any of my neighbors in California.

**Grace:** Wow, that's crazy. Here, it's a small town. So everyone knows everyone.

**Mckenzie:** To me, that's crazy. But I'm looking forward to meeting more people. Everyone seems so nice and friendly here.

**Grace:** They really are. I'll be right back with your sweet tea.

**Mckenzie:** Thanks so much!

## DIALOGUE 102
# Asking for a Raise

**Boss:** So what brings you in today?

**Mira:** Hi. So as you know, I've been working hard for this company for the last two years.

**Boss:** Yes. You've been an amazing employee.

**Mira:** I haven't gotten any raises, so I'm here to request a $3 per hour raise.

**Boss:** That's something I can definitely consider.

**Mira:** Thank you. When do you think you can let me know?

**Boss:** Let me check this quarter's numbers and get back to you by the end of the week.

**Mira:** That would be awesome. I appreciate it.

**Boss:** I appreciate you and all the hard work that you do for this company. Thanks for even asking me for a raise. That must have taken courage.

**Mira:** It did, but I do work with excellence and I feel like the raise is deserved.

**Boss:** Great. Well, is there anything else I can do for you?

**Mira:** Not today. I will look forward to hearing back from you.

**Boss:** Of course. As soon as possible.

**Mira:** Thanks. Enjoy the rest of your day.

**Boss:** You too.

# Ordering Room Service

**Hotel Restaurant:** What can I get for you today?

**Summer:** Hi. I'm calling to order room service.

**Hotel Restaurant:** Okay. What's your room number?

**Summer:** 103

**Hotel Restaurant:** What would you like to order?

**Summer:** Spaghetti with meatballs, a caesar salad with chicken, and the lava cake for dessert.

**Hotel Restaurant:** Would you like vanilla or butter pecan ice cream with your lava cake?

**Summer:** I'll try your butter pecan.

**Hotel Restaurant:** It's my favorite. Any drinks with your order?

**Summer:** Two glasses of your house red wine. Some sparkling water too. Can you bring lemon with that?

**Hotel Restaurant:** Okay. Sure, no problem. We will charge it to your room and it will be up to you in about 40 minutes.

**Summer:** Great. Thanks so much.

**Hotel Restaurant:** Thanks for calling. Enjoy your evening.

## DIALOGUE 104

# Choosing a Gift

**Kelly:** Oh I don't know. It's so hard to decide.

**Lacey:** Well we are in a cute shop there are a lot of choices.

**Kelly:** Jill's birthday is tonight. I don't know why I waited so long to buy her a gift.

**Lacey:** Don't worry. You'll find something. Do you know her hobbies?

**Kelly:** She loves her dog. She also likes to read.

**Lacey:** Look at these adorable journals. Do you think she would like them?

**Kelly:** Maybe. Oh there are also these beautiful earrings. They remind me of her.

**Lacey:** Oh those are pretty.

**Kelly:** This shop also sells some amazing chocolate. Maybe I will get her the earrings and some chocolate bars.

**Lacey:** Maybe I'll get myself some chocolate bars.

**Kelly:** I'm telling you, they are amazing.

**Lacey:** Well I hope you have fun tonight. I wish I could go, but I couldn't get work off.

**Kelly:** I'm sure we'll be hanging out for a while. You should come after work.

**Lacey:** If I'm not too tired!

**Kelly:** Totally. Thanks for coming shopping with me.

**Lacey:** It was fun. I'm happy you found something.

**Kelly:** Me too. I think Jill will love it!

# Leaving a Party

**Titan:** I think we should head home soon.

**Viola:** Really? I'm having so much fun.

**Titan:** I'm exhausted. It's been a long week.

**Viola:** Okay. Well we should find Tim and Sunny to say goodbye.

**Titan:** Speaking of Tim and Sunny, I haven't seen them in awhile.

**Viola:** Strange. It's their party.

**Titan:** Oh there they are. Over in the far corner talking to some other guests.

**Viola:** Maybe we should just sneak out so we don't interrupt their conversation.

**Titan:** I dunno. I think we should at least thank them for hosting.

**Viola:** True. Let's go over there.

**Titan:** Let's try to make it quick. I don't want to get sucked into a long conversation.

**Viola:** Wow, you really are tired aren't you?

**Titan:** Yes. Work stuff was piling up this week. I couldn't catch a break.

**Viola:** Well tomorrow we don't have any plans. You should sleep in.

**Titan:** I plan on it.

# Booking a Taxi to get to the Airport

**Taxi:** Jake's taxi service. How can I help you?

**June:** Hi. I need to schedule a taxi to get to the airport tomorrow morning.

**Taxi:** Which airport?

**June:** Charlotte Douglas.

**Taxi:** Where am I picking you up from?

**June:** I'm staying at the Hilton hotel downtown.

**Taxi:** Okay. What time would you like to be picked up at?

**June:** My flight is at 10am. I think 7:30 will be fine.

**Taxi:** Can I have your name and phone number?

**June:** June Jones. 801-555-0112

**Taxi:** Okay. It will cost $20 to get to the airport from the Hilton.

**June:** That's fine.

**Taxi:** Great. I'll be there in the morning then, 7:30am.

**June:** I'll be waiting. Thank you.

# DIALOGUE 107

# Volunteering

**Liam:** How long have you been volunteering here?

**Anna:** It's going on a year, but I love it.

**Liam:** What exactly is it that you do?

**Anna:** Well this is a retirement home. I come and hang out with the elderly. Sometimes we play cards, sometimes we just chat, and sometimes we walk outside.

**Liam:** That's really cool. Everyone seems to love you here.

**Anna:** I think they see me as a granddaughter.

**Liam:** I imagine so. I'm sure they'll see me as a grandson before long.

**Anna:** Most definitely. So let me introduce you to some of the folks.

**Liam:** Could you show me around the grounds?

**Anna:** Sure. Let's start over here in the living room.

**Liam:** Great. I am actually looking forward to this. I lost my grandma two years ago and I really miss her.

**Anna:** You'll find a lot of sweet people here. Their eyes just light up every time I walk through the door.

**Liam:** That's really sweet. I think I'll like it here.

## DIALOGUE 108

# Discussing Sports

**Jude:** I can't believe the packers lost to the lions.

**Noah:** They haven't been playing very well this season.

**Jude:** I know. It's like they lost their touch.

**Noah:** Did you see that insane tackle right before the endzone?

**Jude:** Yeah, I couldn't believe it. Jones is so fast.

**Noah:** The other guy didn't stand a chance.

**Jude:** Do you think some new guys will be recruited next year?

**Noah:** If they continue to play like this. Maybe they will even get a new quarterback.

**Jude:** That would be a letdown for packer fans.

**Noah:** I think their defense is okay, but man, the offense has to step up their game.

**Jude:** Maybe we should try out for the team.

**Noah:** You're dreaming.

# Driving Lessons

**Bryce:** I'm so nervous.

**Driving instructor:** That's normal. It's your first lesson. But don't worry it will get easier. Just breathe.

**Bryce:** I'm trying, but I'm so nervous that I'm going to mess up.

**Driving instructor:** Just go slow and steady. Be sure to pay attention to stop signs and stop lights.

**Bryce:** Yeah, there is one coming up.

**Driving instructor:** I want you to turn right at the next light.

**Bryce:** Okay, phew, done. My palms are sweaty.

**Driving instructor:** Just continue to keep your eyes on the road and your hands on the wheel.

**Bryce:** Oh no, it's starting to rain.

**Driving instructor:** You can turn on your car lights and the windshield wipers. Good.

**Bryce:** Just my luck that it started to rain.

**Driving instructor:** No worries. Okay, I'm going to have you practice parallel parking right up there.

**Bryce:** I'm glad there are no other cars around.

**Driving instructor:** Just be sure to put your blinker on. Ease in slowly.

**Bryce:** I can't believe I did it.

**Driving instructor:** You did a great job. I'll see you again on Thursday.

**Bryce:** Thanks so much.

# The Apology

**Dad:** So what happened son?

**Maddox:** I'm so sorry. We were playing baseball. I didn't think that I would break the window.

**Dad:** So it was you or one of your friends?

**Maddox:** One of my friends pitched me the ball, I was the one who hit it.

**Dad:** I see. Well, accidents happen. Can you get the broom?

**Maddox:** Yeah, I'll help clean it up. Do I have to pay for it?

**Dad:** Since you told me the truth and it was an accident, don't worry. I won't take it out of your allowance. But I suggest that you play farther away from the house next time.

**Maddox:** Yeah, we'll go a block away to that open field near our house.

**Dad:** That's a good idea. Be careful not to cut yourself on this glass.

**Maddox:** I will. Thanks for helping me clean up dad. Again, I'm sorry.

**Dad:** It's okay son. Now let's finish cleaning this up before your mom gets home.

# Congratulations!

You did it! 110 real life dialogues in English. Wasn't that fun? I'm proud of you. I encourage you to go back through the book again. Role play, practice these conversations out loud. Language learning is a journey. I believe that repetition is a key to success. The more times you come in contact with certain words and phrases, the more that they will become second nature to you. Don't forget to write some notes in the blank pages that follow. If you want to study even further with this book you can purchase the companion guide that explains 223 English expressions used in the book.

**If you enjoyed this book, please write me a review. I would love your feedback.**

**Don't forget to find me on social media:**

**Instagram** @camillehanson

**Tiktok** @learnenglishwithcamille

**Youtube** @learnenglishwithcamille

**Check out my other English Book!**

# Short Travel Stories for English Learners

Available in Extended English Version and Parallel Versions for:

- Spanish

- Turkish

- Portuguese

- French

- Italian

**VISIT LEARNENGLISHWITHCAMILLE.COM**

# NOTES

Made in United States
Orlando, FL
15 September 2023

36989437R00068